DIGGER

THE TRAGIC FATE OF THE CALIFORNIA INDIANS FROM THE MISSIONS TO THE GOLD RUSH

JERRY STANLEY

CROWN PUBLISHERS, INC.
New York

Text copyright © 1997 by Jerry Stanley
Maps copyright © 1997 by Christy Hale

Published by Crown Publishers, Inc., a Random House company,
201 East 50th Street, New York, New York 10022

CROWN is a trademark of Crown Publishers, Inc.

http://www.randomhouse.com/

Printed in the United States of America

Library of Congress Cataloging-in-Publication Data
Stanley, Jerry, 1941–
Digger : the tragic fate of the California Indians from the missions
to the gold rush / Jerry Stanley. — 1st ed.
p. cm.
Includes bibliographical references and index.
1. Indians of North America—California—Juvenile literature. 2. Indians of North America—
Missions—California—Juvenile literature. 3. Gold mines and mining—California—Juvenile literature. California—Antiquities—Juvenile literature. I. Title.
E78.C15S8   1997
979.4'01—dc21   96-48225

ISBN   0-517-70951-1 (trade)
0-517-70952-X (lib. bdg.)

10 9 8 7 6 5 4 3 2 1

FIRST EDITION

Picture credits follow the index.

For Simon Boughton

CONTENTS

INTRODUCTION

IN 1769 FATHER JUNIPERO SERRA, a Franciscan priest, left Mexico for San Diego with the goal of converting California Indians to the Catholic religion and the Spanish way of life. Serra entered San Diego wearing a long brown robe and riding a mule. He was accompanied by Spanish soldiers who wore leather breastplates, and by other men who carried supplies and who, like the soldiers, had beards. The local Indians hid in the bushes and tried to make sense of the strange creatures.

The Indians had never seen a mule before, and it seemed to them that Serra was part human and part animal. The creatures with leather chests looked like beetles wrapped in hard shells. The creatures with hairy faces appeared to be bears, or part bear and part human. Whatever they were, they possessed powerful magic: they had no women and could somehow multiply without them. Serra was encased in a brown tube, and when he dismounted and walked away from the mule it appeared that he had no arms or legs. But somehow he could walk and carry two sticks that were fastened in the shape of a cross.

Serra climbed a hill, planted the wooden cross, and shouted, "Come, o come, and receive the Faith!" The Indians couldn't understand the Spanish words or the meaning of the crossed sticks. Kneeling on the ground, his arms raised, Serra cried out again, "Come, o come, and receive the Faith!" The Indians watched to see what would happen next. Eventually the man stopped shouting and walked down from the hill. He was joined

1

by other brown tubes and some of the beetles. Carrying food and trinkets, the party started walking toward the bushes, but before they reached the Indians' hiding place, the Indians ran away. The soldiers mounted horses and gave chase. The Indians were brought back to the site of the cross and put to work building a mission, where they were forced to live and learn the Spanish way of life. The tragedy of the California Indians had begun.

Eighty years after Serra arrived in San Diego, gold was discovered in California. Starting in 1849, Americans by the thousands traveled west to join the California gold rush. That same year miners from Oregon were digging for gold near the northern California town of Marysville when they spotted an Indian family using sticks to dig for wild carrots. The miners likened the Indians to hogs rooting in the dirt. They shouted that the Indians should leave.

When the Indians seemed to hesitate, one of the miners shouted, "Digger! Digger!" as he fired his rifle in the air. The Indians ran away, knowing that if they stayed they might be shot.

Both the Spanish and the Americans who arrived in California believed their way of life, their culture, was superior to the California Indians'. Culture is the way people dress, the ideas they believe in, their art, their language, their whole way of life. Like all people everywhere, California Indians had their own religion, government, art, music, and sports, and their culture was the most precious gift they possessed—the way they chose to live. But the Spanish and the Americans didn't understand this, and the result was the near extinction of a way of life that started in California 12,000 years ago.

This is the story of the California Indians and their struggle to survive.

PART I
THE NATURAL WORLD OF THE CALIFORNIA INDIANS

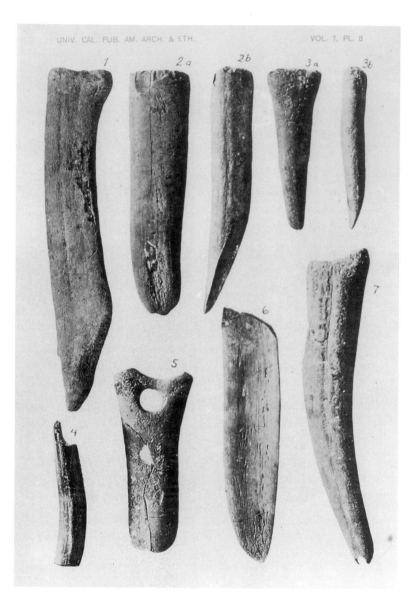

The first people entered California about 10,000 B.C., following and
hunting vast herds of animals. These ornaments and hunting implements,
made from bone and antler and dating from prehistoric times, were
collected at an archaeological site in the San Francisco Bay area.

THE FIRST CALIFORNIANS 1

LIKE OTHER NATIVE AMERICANS, the people who became California Indians made a long journey from southern Asia to the New World about 14,000 years ago. Previously, huge glaciers covered much of the earth, but these glaciers started to melt about 20,000 B.C., first in southern Asia, then, farther north, in Siberia. As the glaciers receded, they were replaced by thousands of miles of grassland where enormous herds of animals grazed. The people from southern Asia followed these herds northward and became hunters.

They hunted huge bison and woolly mammoth twice the size of the elephants of today. They invented bows and arrows to improve their chances of a successful hunt, for if they did not take an animal once a week, they would die. They always had to be prepared to move at a moment's notice to follow the herds, but if they got too close they might be killed in a stampede. Wolves and terrifying saber-toothed tigers also hunted the herd animals, and would attack people who got in the way. To watch out for the dreaded tigers and hunt more successfully, families formed tribes, communities of people who hunted together and protected one another. Slugging it out with the great beasts every day, these tough, courageous people became smarter because of the knowledge that came from humans cooperating and sharing. For 8,000 years, they followed the herds north, not knowing where their journey would end.

By 12,000 B.C. the glaciers had receded far enough to uncover a

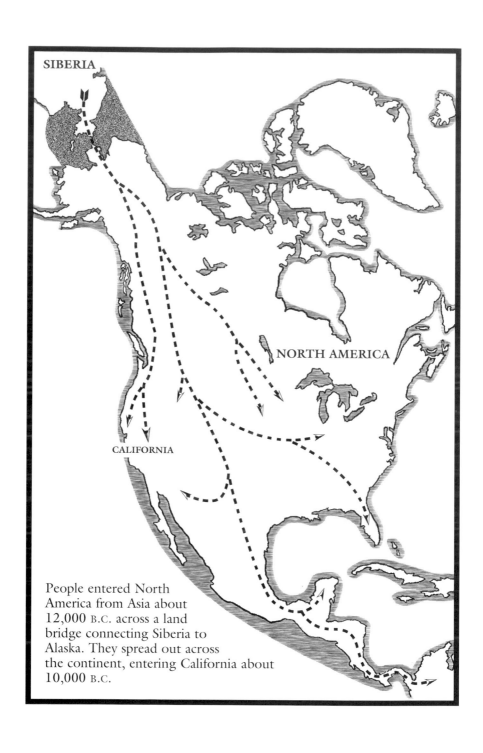

SIBERIA

NORTH AMERICA

CALIFORNIA

People entered North
America from Asia about
12,000 B.C. across a land
bridge connecting Siberia to
Alaska. They spread out across
the continent, entering California about
10,000 B.C.

land bridge connecting Siberia to Alaska. But because the ice was melting and the ocean was rising, the land bridge lasted only 500 years, then disappeared below the sea. Arriving in Siberia at just the right moment, animals crossed the land bridge; people followed them; and then the bridge was covered by the ocean. Although they did not know they had entered another continent, the people who walked to the New World soon found they were in a paradise.

North and South America were teeming with birds, flowers, fish—and immense herds of bison and mammoth. Much earlier, about 40,000 B.C., there had been another land bridge between Siberia and Alaska, and it had carried a wide variety of animals to the New World. Their numbers had been increasing for years when the hunters of 12,000 B.C. encountered them.

With plenty of food everywhere they looked, the tribes fanned out across America, their populations growing fast. They would become the Cheyenne, Sioux, Cherokee, and the other peoples of North America. Others went to Mexico and South America and grew into the great nations of the Aztecs, Incas, and Mayas. When the European explorers arrived in A.D. 1500, there were not just a few people living in the New World but more than 2,000 separate cultures. How many people lived in the New World in 1500 isn't known, but researchers have concluded that perhaps as many as 90 million were living in the New World and 10 million were living in the area that later became the United States. So bountiful was the food supply and so spacious was the land that the native population in the New World was larger than that of all European nations combined.

The travelers from Asia almost missed settling California. Hemmed in by mountains, deserts, and ocean, California was a difficult place to enter. As a result, Native Americans at first bypassed the region for more suitable areas; they had settled much of the New World before they entered California, in about 10,000 B.C. Seeking escape from the hunt and searching for new grazing lands, some Ice Age animals had made their way through the mountain passes in northern California; they were followed by the first Californians. Five separate groups of people came from the north, and another group entered southern California through what is now Arizona and Mexico. There were six distinct language families spoken in Native California: Algonquin, Athabascan, Penutian, Hokan, Uto-Aztecan, and Yukian.

Once the animals and the people made it through the mountains to the interior valleys of the state, there was no turning back: the barriers that had kept them out for so long now kept them in. As they hiked into the new territory, they were unaware that they were about to become the luckiest Indians in the New World.

THE CULTURES OF THE CALIFORNIA INDIANS 2

PROBABLY THERE NEVER WAS a more beautiful and bountiful place than California about 10,000 B.C. It had rivers where salmon spawned two, even three, times a year. It had mountains with otter, beaver, elk, deer, moose, and bighorn sheep. It had grasslands with rabbits. It had meadows with antelope. It had forests, it had deserts, and it had its own ocean with fin fish, shellfish, crabs, sea otters, and whales. Most important of all, it had the largest valley in the world, the great San Joaquin, which contained over 500 different edible plants, including blackberries, melons, and sprawling orchards of acorn-bearing trees. The soil was so rich and the climate so perfect that plants bore three times a year instead of just once. And there was no one there.

By 7000 B.C. the five groups that had entered the state from the north occupied most parts of California where there were animals to hunt. For the first 3,000 years, until about 7000 B.C., the California Indians paid little attention to all the plant food in the state and how it might be harvested. For thousands of years, they had lived by hunting the big Ice Age mammals, and there was no reason to change. They were foragers, not gatherers: if they found some berries, they ate them, but they did not prepare the berries, store the berries, or know when or where to find ripe berries.

By 7000 B.C. the hunters had wiped out thirty-one species of animals, including the giant sloth, the mammoth, the mastodon, and even the horse. Now that the animals were lost forever, the California Indians had to change to survive. Accordingly, they

Hunting animals and collecting wild foods such as berries and acorns sustained the native peoples of California. These arrows and woven bags were made by northern California Indians: the arrows and the bag above are Yurok. The bags below are Maidu.

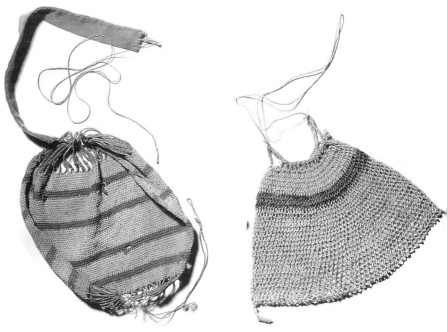

established permanent settlements throughout the state and lived in separate groups. By the time Europeans came to the Americas there were about a hundred different California Indian tribes.

Through trial and error and much experimentation over thousands of years, they devised different ways of living with nature instead of destroying it. No matter where they settled in the state, they became experts at adapting to the environment, and each group developed a unique culture that arose from that environment. They studied nature and lived according to what they saw and felt in their natural world. They were successful in that they lived in one place for 12,000 years without much hunger or starvation.

This success came because they shared with one another and were caretakers of nature. This was the main idea in their cultures. Whatever the various tribes did   catch salmon, like the Hupa in the northwest; hunt deer, like the Modoc in the northeast; gather seeds, like the Mono in the southern desert; spear seals, like the Chumash on the coast; grow beans, like the Yuma along the Colorado River; harvest acorns, like the Yokuts in the San Joaquin Valley—they were careful to leave enough for others and enough so nature could replenish itself. They believed that God was in every living thing, and they took care to thank the Great Spirit for providing them with food and allowing them to live.

Camping on the banks of the Klamath River in the spring, the Yurok fasted and prayed to the Great Spirit for the return of the salmon. Waiting farther upstream, the Hupa, Shasta, and Wiyot were doing the same thing. They knew when the salmon were due to return to the river and spawn, but their knowledge did not make them superior to the salmon, and they took care to show this. Like their grandparents, who had passed on this knowledge, they understood that it was a mistake to take salmon

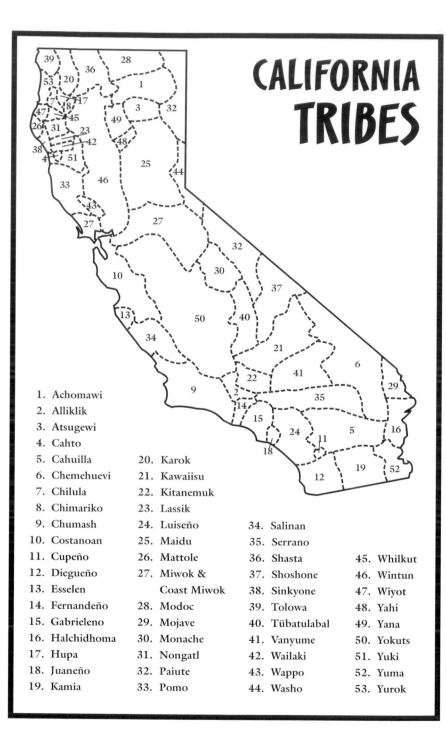

CALIFORNIA TRIBES

1. Achomawi
2. Alliklik
3. Atsugewi
4. Cahto
5. Cahuilla
6. Chemehuevi
7. Chilula
8. Chimariko
9. Chumash
10. Costanoan
11. Cupeño
12. Diegueño
13. Esselen
14. Fernandeño
15. Gabrieleno
16. Halchidhoma
17. Hupa
18. Juaneño
19. Kamia
20. Karok
21. Kawaiisu
22. Kitanemuk
23. Lassik
24. Luiseño
25. Maidu
26. Mattole
27. Miwok & Coast Miwok
28. Modoc
29. Mojave
30. Monache
31. Nongatl
32. Paiute
33. Pomo
34. Salinan
35. Serrano
36. Shasta
37. Shoshone
38. Sinkyone
39. Tolowa
40. Tübatulabal
41. Vanyume
42. Wailaki
43. Wappo
44. Washo
45. Whilkut
46. Wintun
47. Wiyot
48. Yahi
49. Yana
50. Yokuts
51. Yuki
52. Yuma
53. Yurok

from the river just because they could, and also a mistake not to show thanks to the salmon.

Firm in believing that they were only one part of the design in nature, the Yurok would choose a person of great respect to take a single fish from the river. That fish was used to conduct the First Salmon Ceremony. While gently passing the fish around from hand to hand, each member examined it carefully and in a whisper thanked it for looking so good, which would please the mysterious force that sustained life. After an hour of praise, the salmon was carefully cooked, then cut into as many pieces as there were people for a feast of thanks. The skeleton of the fish was returned to the river with its head facing upstream so the other salmon would continue swimming upstream. Only then were baskets and fish traps placed in the river to provide food for the next three months. First the Yurok, then the Hupa and Shasta, let enough salmon pass so the others upstream could take their catch.

At dawn on a high plateau in northern California, men of the Modoc and Atsugewi said good-bye to their wives and children and went to prepare for the hunt. They would not see their families during the three days of isolation required before taking a deer, nor would they eat anything. With bow and arrows and sharpened stones for cutting and scraping, each walked silently to the far end of the village, then disappeared into the sweat lodge, an airtight hut built into the ground. During each of the three days in the lodge, they built a fire under stones until the stones became red-hot. Splashed with water, the stones produced steam to make the men sweat while they sang to the deer, prayed to its spirit, and prepared their weapons. Dripping with heavy sweat, each ran from the lodge to a nearby stream and plunged in, then ran back for a sweat and back to the river, five, six times a day for three days, until their bodies were pure and they could meet the deer.

To be in harmony with their prey, and so they wouldn't be seen, the men wore deer heads and crept through the grass until they were close enough to crouch and fire an arrow. If the hunt was successful, the deer was cleaned where it fell, and once again thanks were offered. A successful hunter gained honor and won favor from everyone, but among the Modoc and other hunting tribes the hunter ate little of his prey. Instead, he gave most of it to family and friends to show that he was generous and didn't need the meat. Such a great hunter could easily take another deer whenever he wanted.

Farther south in the San Joaquin Valley, the Yokuts gathered in the center of their village when the oak trees were heavy with acorns. The Miwok, Maidu, and Costanoan were doing the same. For one full week in the fall they danced and prayed day and night, hardly sleeping, to thank the Great Spirit for the sacred acorn. Except for the grandparents tending infants, the entire village made the five-mile walk to the foothills where the oak trees grew.

Each tribe had its own oak grove, but often three different tribes worked side by side in the same orchard, Yokuts, Monache, and Miwok sharing the bounty and respecting their neighbors. Young boys climbed the trees and shook the acorns loose while men on the ground used poles to poke the branches, and women gathered the crop. Because they took care not to damage the trees, the oaks produced food every fall. One tribe's oak grove could yield over 100,000 pounds of acorns, enough food for three years!

After hauling the crop back to the village in cone-shaped baskets, Yokuts women prepared the food in a most ingenious way. The raw acorns contained acid and tasted awful, but the California Indians had figured out a way to get rid of this acid.

The caps were snapped off and a hand-held milling stone was used to crack the nuts open and grind the meal into small particles that looked like sand. The women then poured water through the meal for hours to leach out the acid and make the meal sweet. Next, the meal was cooked in watertight baskets, using hot stones to boil it, and then berries were added to make the daily stew. The rest was made into bread, enough for several days. Only the California Indians knew how the acorn could be made edible. In other parts of America where oak trees grew, people never did figure out the secret of the acorn.

California Indians also learned that it was a mistake to rely on just one source of food. The farming tribes of the southeastern United States—the Cherokee, Choctaw, and Creek—experienced famines when there was a drought or too much rain. But wherever a California Indian called home, there were at least two different things to eat, and usually ten or twelve. Of course, for each there was a ceremony: the Pomo sang for the arrival of clover; the Hupa danced before taking the first eel in the spring; the Wappo prayed at the return of gooseberries.

Clever people, and lucky because of the bounty of California, most of the tribes occupied regions that included at least two different environments. When they weren't stalking deer in the mountains, the Modoc were gathering berries at a lower elevation. When they weren't collecting acorns in a meadow, the Yokuts were spearing whitefish in a river. The Miwok dug for the bulbs of the desert lily, which they baked like potatoes, but they also hiked into the mountains, where they attracted bighorn sheep by banging rocks together to mimic the sound of rams fighting. The Mojave grew corn, but also hunted antelope. The Chumash fished, but also gathered blackberries. And when they grew tired of eating cactus, the desert-dwelling Cahuilla moved to their second home, a valley north of San Diego where they could eat fruit and small game. Another desert-dwelling tribe, the southwestern Pomo, liked acorns, but didn't have any oak trees where they lived. They solved the problem by following the woodpecker, and when he wasn't looking, they stole his stash of acorns.

Feasting on a nutritious diet of meat, fish, and plants, and sharing with one another, the Yurok, Modoc, and other tribes increased their populations for thousands of years. When the Europeans arrived in California, the local population was about 400,000 and it was still on the rise. There were more Indians living in California than in any other part of what is now the United States. With nature as their guide, they made a home for themselves, and when they weren't fishing and gathering, they spent most of their time just having fun.

THE WAY OF THE 3
CALIFORNIA INDIANS

THE CALIFORNIA INDIANS' DAY was not divided into eight hours of work, eight hours of sleep, and eight hours of play. If there were acorns to harvest, the Yahi harvested acorns and did little else, including sleep. During salmon runs, the Shasta fished for as long as it took to secure their supply, then moved on to do other things. Only the farming tribes along the Colorado River tended the same fields for months at a time, but even they stopped farm work when the growing season stopped. The rhythm of nature told the California Indians what they should do each day and they did not distinguish between what might be called "work" and doing nothing at all. They did not consider gathering acorns work, like a job. It was just something they occasionally did, and there was little difference between gathering acorns and swimming in a stream. Life was life.

The California Indians organized their societies in one of three ways. Some resembled the Yurok along the northern coast: they had no single ruler, and instead the men of wealth made decisions for the tribe. Others resembled the Yuma along the Colorado River: they lived in bands of about 135 people and each band was led by a headman. However, the most common form of organization was the tribelet, a collection of villages whose people spoke the same dialect of a particular language. More than half of all California Indians lived in tribelets.

There were about 500 tribelets in California. They ranged in size from fifty to 2,000 people, and each was guided by a head-

A collection of
California Indian
baskets, from the
Pomo and other
northern California
tribes. Indians
throughout
California were
skilled craftspeople;
the Pomo, in
particular, were
famous for their
baskets, which were
so tightly woven
that they could
hold water.

man, or chief. Unlike the Sioux, Cheyenne, and other Native American tribes, the chief was not chosen because he was a great warrior, nor was he given much power. He was picked for his skill as a provider, and his main job was to make sure everyone had enough to eat. He had to be honest and not selfish, and it helped if he was a good dancer for the many ceremonies held to give thanks to the Great Spirit. To show respect, members of the tribelet gave him food and blankets, but he gave this wealth back whenever anyone needed anything. He lost his job almost immediately if the oak trees failed to bear or the deer were scarce. The chief of the Natchez tribe in Louisiana could put people to death for no reason at all. The chief of a California tribelet offered advice, and if anyone thought it was bad advice, they ignored him.

Except for the Colorado River tribes, the California Indians mostly lived in peace with one another. Different from the other tribes in many ways, the Colorado River tribes—the Yuma, Mojave, Diegueño, and Cahuilla—evolved from people who entered California from the south after 3000 B.C. and whose languages belonged principally to the Uto-Aztecan family. They were the only farmers in the state, though not the only ones who knew how to farm. The Tolowa knew about farming but chose to fish instead. The Yana knew about planting but preferred to tend oak groves. Farming was hard work, and in California it was associated with war because of the warlike nature of the farming tribes. Each had a warrior class whose job it was to attack the other farming tribes, kill and scalp their warriors, and enslave their women and children, who were kept as proof of victory. They traveled as far away as 150 miles for a fight and they believed that war enhanced the spiritual nature of the tribe as a whole.

Among the nonfarming tribes, disputes were settled quickly and most of the time peacefully. If Miwok trespassed on a Yokuts oak grove, the two chiefs met and negotiated a time and place for justice. Members of the tribelets stood on grass hills opposite each other, cheering for their side; below them stood two lines of men. The men faced each other at a respectful distance of a hundred feet or so and shouted insults back and forth for an allotted time; then arrows were drawn and the fight was on. It lasted no more than a few minutes. Volleys of arrows rained down on each side until someone was hit, and then the bows were thrown to the ground. If a Chumash tribelet charged another Chumash tribelet with giving inferior gifts during a ceremony, the two sides squared off for a game of shinny, a rough-and-tumble version of modern-day soccer played with a ball made of hide and stuffed with deer hair. Instead of firing arrows or playing a sport, the Wintun and Wiyot agreed that paying a fine was enough to settle any conflict. Except for the farming tribes, the California Indians didn't have the rage for fighting, and it was unthinkable for one tribelet to kill members of another tribelet and steal its land. But punishment for a misdeed within the tribelet—for example, stealing from a neighbor—was the most horrible thing imaginable: banishment from the tribelet, friends, and family—in effect, from life itself.

The way of the California Indian was to show humility to the Great Spirit and to each other in most daily activities. One way to show humility was in giving and receiving gifts. If a Miwok was the first to be hit by an arrow in a dispute with Yokuts, peace was restored by the Yokuts giving gifts to the Miwok. The winner at shinny was expected to give gifts to the loser. Showing humility by being unselfish was also important in gambling, a favorite pastime of California Indians. The Salinan used seashells in the same way as playing cards. The Wappo tossed handfuls of sticks in the air and bet on whether the number of sticks was odd or even. The Yahi bet on which hand held the pebble. While betting, they sang gambling songs, made fun of one another, and played practical jokes. But once the game was over, they went back to showing humility. Winners never bragged, losers never complained, and winners were expected to return a portion of their proceeds to the losers. This was especially true when tribelets met.

At the start of their World Renewal Ceremony for the acorn, the chief and elders of a Yokuts tribelet would welcome the members of a Monache tribelet with gifts, and would receive gifts in return. For the serious business of gift giving, each group sat in its own circle, passed the items around, and compared their value to the value of what they had given: shell-bead money; surplus fish; watermelon bartered from the Mojave; asphaltum bartered from the Chumash, for making glue; obsidian for arrow tips; flint for starting fires; pottery; baskets; and diapers made from rabbit fur. Some of the items had been traded five or six times along the extensive trails that threaded throughout California. Although the California Indians spoke six different languages and over a hundred different dialects and couldn't always understand one another, they understood the value of trade items.

The Monache, assessing the gifts, might decide that the Yokuts had given substandard baskets and ought to add more shell beads to make the gifts' value even. With satisfaction achieved, the tribelets moved on to other matters: trading, gambling, swapping stories, playing shinny, and eventually conducting the World Renewal Ceremony.

The meeting of two tribelets was also an opportunity to find a mate, and as young men and women introduced themselves to one another there was much talk about the gifts that would be needed for the marriages and much betting on which couples were likely to wed. The California Indians married in their teenage years, and if a marriage wasn't working, divorce was simple. For example, infertility was cause for the husband to place his wife's personal belongings—baskets, clothing, milling stones—outside the hut as a signal that the marriage was over. Being a poor provider caused the husband to get kicked out. In the case of the husband's death, his brother was expected to marry the widow and provide for her, even if he already had a wife. He willingly assumed responsibility for her and kept his thoughts to himself. He was such a great man that he could provide for a hundred wives. He was showing this, and he didn't need to say it.

The way of the California Indian was not to boast or draw attention to oneself. This was a part of sharing, gift-giving, and everyday life. When elders of a tribelet discussed matters of importance, such as when to move to higher ground, clowns were hired to interrupt the speakers and mock them to discount the importance of any one person. This humility even extended to a California Indian's name. Naming ceremonies often went on for hours, with dozens of names discussed before one was chosen. But once a name was chosen, it was rarely ever spoken again, and never was it called out to gain individual attention. California Indians referred to each other indirectly and never spoke of the dead by name. To them, the individual was less important than the family, the village, the people, and their place in the plan of life.

The values of restraint, humility, and unselfishness were passed on to children in stories told around the campfire at night. A main figure in these tales was called Coyote. Coyote represented humans and was used to show that people can make mistakes if they disregard the design in nature. According to one tale, all the stars in the sky used to be spaced in neat rows, but a foolish act by Coyote left them horribly disarranged. In another story, Coyote did not follow the rules for hunting and ended up being the hunted. The storyteller was an older man who knew the tribe's folklore, and as he told the story he acted out each character with gestures to convey joy, greed, wisdom, and error.

California Indians did go hungry when droughts destroyed their food supply. Sometimes they fought bloody wars, usually over charges of witchcraft. And, like all societies, theirs included thieves, cheats, and murderers. But typically life for the California Indians was easy and fun.

They didn't wear much clothing because it wasn't needed. They lived in temporary villages, which enabled them to move and keep their diet healthy. If disease hit a tribelet and no cure could be found, they burned their village, moved to another site, and started again. Their shamans, or doctors, used elk clover to heal sores, buckhorn cholla to soothe burns, and milfoil for stomachaches, colds, and sore eyes. One-fourth of all the medicines developed in the United States come from the hundreds of plants Native Americans used.

During a typical day Yokuts women sat in circles near a group of huts weaving baskets and talking about their families. Modoc men visited the sweat lodge, made arrows, and reminisced about a great hunt and why they were so blessed that day. When he missed a shot, a hunter said, "The deer didn't want to die for me today," and the others nodded in agreement. Children swam in the rivers, ran through the grass, and played games. Grandparents talked about their grandchildren, while the chief watched the moon and calculated when to move the tribelet. During a typical day, California Indians made some things they needed—baskets, bows, and canoes—but mostly they ate, slept, gambled, played, and made love.

And then a ship appeared on the horizon where none had been seen before. On board was a man who wore a robe of thorns that dug into his skin. He used candles to burn his arms and legs. He pounded his chest with a large stone. At night he whipped himself on the back with a chain of iron spikes and cried out, "Sinner! Sinner!" Holding a large cross high in the air, he was accompanied to shore by men with guns.

PART II
THE MISSIONS

Ceremonial dance headdresses worn by northern California Indians near San Francisco. This engraving was made from an illustration by Ludovik Choris, who visited northern California in 1816 as part of a Russian naval expedition. Traditional Indian costume like this, outlawed by missionaries trying to convert Indians to the Spanish way of life, would soon be lost from California.

Mission San Gabriel, 1832.
This painting, dating from
the end of the mission era,
shows religious observances
taking place outside the
mission and, in the
foreground, the kind of
domed thatch house built by
many southern California
Indians. The peaceful image
it presents is misleading:
local Indians, called
Gabrielenos by the Spanish,
were rounded up by armed
soldiers and forced to work
in mission workshops and on
mission farms.

THE ARRIVAL OF THE SPANISH **4**

THE DIEGUEÑO OF SAN DIEGO were the first people in California to see the white-winged bird that carried the strange creatures ashore. In 1542 the explorer Juan Rodriguez Cabrillo, who was in the service of Spain, anchored in the bay of San Diego, led his men ashore, and ruined the Diegu   eño's food supply by camping in their garden. Had he asked the chief for permission, the party would have been taken to the campground reserved for visitors. Without asking, Cabrillo's men killed squirrels, rabbits, and deer that belonged to the tribe, but they did pay for some fish with beads and cloth.

The Spanish were looking for a shortcut to India, and for gold in a mythical place called the Seven Cities of Cibola. Like other tribes living along the coast, the Dieguño had heard about creatures who lived far to the south, but when the Spanish came ashore wearing leather breastplates and beards, the Indians weren't sure if they were humans, animals, or insects. Since there were no females in the group, they looked like a hunting party, or a war party. They certainly did not come to trade.

They were astoundingly rude, using their fingers to point at the Dieguño and draw attention to individual people. They were filthy and smelled something awful, because they didn't bathe daily and didn't coat their bodies with minerals to stay free of sores and insects as the Dieguño did. They must have been driven from their own land, because all of them were thieves. The Chumash of Santa Barbara thought much the same thing when Cabrillo visited there. Sharing food with the Spanish, they were friendly until it was clear they were to receive nothing in return. Then the Chumash became cold and distant and skirmished with the sailors over the winter's supply of cured fish.

Following Cabrillo's expedition, there was only occasional contact between Europeans and the California Indians for the next hundred years. In 1579 the English adventurer Sir Francis Drake spent five weeks exploring Bodega Bay; the Coast Miwok were sometimes friendly and sometimes not. In 1587 Pedro de Unamuno visited Morro Bay; the Costanoan were sometimes friendly and sometimes not, depending on the manners of the visitors. In 1595 Sebastian Rodriguez Cermeno anchored in San Francisco Bay as the Coast Miwok crowded the beach and watched cautiously. One launched a boat made of reeds and paddled out to the ship; he returned with cloth and a red cap. Four more paddled out the next day and returned with similar gifts. This was suitable generosity.

As soon as the Miwok left the beach, Cermeno went ashore with twenty-two armed men. They built a fort, took Miwok food without asking, and claimed the land for the king of Spain. A priest was along and he christened the land for the Catholic church. After a month the Spanish prepared to leave, having secured enough food to continue their voyage. But a storm wrecked their ship and destroyed the food. The Miwok escorted the Spanish party inland, where they bartered with another tribelet for enough acorns to complete the trip to Mexico. These were strange creatures indeed. They knew how to build a boat of great size, but they took whatever they wanted from nature and from others without asking.

After Cermeno's voyage, the Spanish temporarily lost interest in California. Since arriving in the New World at the end of the fifteenth century, the Spanish had moved through most of South America, seizing land and building missions to convert the Indians. When the Indians resisted, they were shot or driven into the mountains and deserts, where many starved to death. The Aztecs of Lake Texcoco in Mexico fought for three months, living on rats and mice before they fell to the Spanish conquistador Hernando Cortes in 1521. The Maya towns along the Yucatan peninsula fought the Spanish conquest until they fell in 1540. Carried to South America from Cuba, smallpox moved with the invading forces through Peru, Argentina, and Chile, killing entire nations of Native Americans who had no immunity to the disease. The Spanish found large deposits of gold and silver in Mexico and Peru, but the cost to the native population was high. When the Spanish arrived in the New World, at least 30 million people lived in the lands south of California. By 1769, there were only about 4 million.

The European nations claimed they had the right to take land away from the Native Americans because they were "uncivilized": they wore little clothing, did not farm, and did not know God and his Son, Jesus Christ. Spain and the other countries that took over the New World did not value the culture of the Indians they met. When Christopher Columbus returned to Spain after visiting America, he brought back some Indians—not to show his queen that people living in different parts of the world have different cultures, but to show her that the natives were "uncivilized" and therefore Spain would be justified in taking their land. But, the Spanish believed, the Indians could be made "civilized"—if they would adopt Spanish ways.

Accordingly, in 1769 the Spanish sent two land parties and three supply ships to California. Led by Captain Gaspar de Portola, the governor of Baja California, and Junipero Serra, a

Franciscan priest, this so-called "sacred expedition" had two aims: to claim the land for Spain, which feared that Russia might take the territory, and to convert the California Indians. The force included about 300 men in all. About half were soldiers, and there were five priests in the group. The rest were black-smiths, carpenters, bakers, cooks, and muleteers. As was custom-ary in founding new establishments, a number of Christianized Indians from Mexico were taken along to induce the California Indians to a new way of life. The first step was to establish a set-tlement and a mission in what is now San Diego.

Captain Fernando Rivera y Moncada headed one land party, which included cavalry soldiers who were also skilled as cowboys. Driving a large herd of cattle, horses, and mules, Rivera's group left Baja on March 24. Portola and Serra headed the second land party, which left on May 15, following the trail left by Rivera. Before them, in January and February, the three supply ships—the *San Antonio*, the *San Carlos*, and the *San Jose*—had set sail from San Blas, Mexico. They carried books, tools, trade items, food, and religious articles: bells, hymnals, and musical instruments.

The *San Antonio* was the first to arrive, on April 11, after an easy voyage of fifty-four days. Although the *San Carlos* had start-ed first, a month earlier than the *San Antonio,* she encountered severe storms and spent 110 days at sea before reaching San Diego almost three weeks behind the *San Antonio.* Nearly all her men had scurvy, a disease caused by the lack of vitamin C, and most had lost their teeth. Twenty-four had died at sea, and the survivors were so weak from malnutrition that none had the strength to lower a boat to the water for the trip to shore. The *San Antonio*'s crew had to board the *San Carlos* and bring them ashore. The first Spanish settlement in California was a makeshift hospital on the beach, a tent fashioned from one of the sails of the *San Carlos*. As for the *San Jose*, she fared worst of all, being lost at sea with all hands somewhere on the way to San Diego.

During the 350-mile trip through the parched deserts of Baja, Rivera's party made up for dwindling food supplies by carefully trading cloth for food with Indians they met along the way. When they arrived, on May 14, Rivera ordered the settlement moved seven miles north to the foot of a hill where a presidio, a fort, would later be built. Portola rode in with his men on June 29, and Serra reached the camp on July 1.

Nearly all the Christianized Indians who had been brought along had died or deserted; the military officers denied them rations when food ran low. Of the 300 men in the "sacred expedition," not more than half survived to reach San Diego, and most of the survivors were too sick to work for months. During the trip, Serra himself suffered much pain from a leg ulcer until it was treated with herbs and a mud pack. Nevertheless, he was happy to see that the other priests had arrived safely: Fathers Juan Viscaino, Fernando Parron, Francis Gomez, and Juan Crespi. On July 2 they celebrated mass in honor of the reunion, and after resting for a few weeks, on July 16 Serra climbed Presidio Hill, planted a cross, and shouted, "Come, o come, and receive the Faith!" The Diegueño watched from the bushes.

A man of great faith, a man who beat his chest with a rock and whipped himself at night because he believed it would keep him free of sin, Father Junipero Serra was a person of goodwill. He and the others did not come to California to kill the Indians; they came to improve the lives of the Indians and save their souls. Like the other missionaries, Serra believed he was ordered by God to spread the Gospel of Jesus Christ, and if he failed to do this, his own soul was in peril. He soon learned that saving the Indians would not be an easy task.

When Serra shouted, "Come and receive the Faith!" the Diegueño were unable to understand his words or what he wanted. When he and the soldiers approached, the Diegueño ran away, fearing what they did not understand.

This same problem with communication arose in establishing other missions. For months and even years, depending on the mission and the local dialect, language difficulties prevented the priests from winning converts. Six months passed before Serra could learn enough Diegueño words to communicate, but in January 1770 his spirits were raised when an Indian baby was offered for baptism, his first convert. His joy turned to disappointment when the Indians suddenly snatched the child from his arms and ran off before the ceremony could be completed. Miscommunication and misunderstanding were powerful barriers separating the two cultures.

Undaunted, Serra proceeded with the building of Mission San Diego, the first mission, and he established the pattern for how the other missions started and grew. Spanish workers constructed the first buildings: huts of tule (a kind of tall reed) for the priests and the workers, a presidio for the soldiers. While the priests learned the Indians' language, packet ships from Mexico arrived every three months or so, carrying additional workers, soldiers, food, and supplies, strengthening the settlement.

Having learned some of their language, Serra encouraged the Diegueño to build their huts near the settlement, and if they agreed to help build the mission, he gave them gifts of cloth and food. First a dozen, then a few dozen more, accepted the gifts and were put to work making adobe bricks and fashioning pine beams to fortify the wall surrounding the mission. The Indians also constructed the permanent buildings inside: the church; workshops; storage rooms; and living quarters for the priests, the

Indians, and the Spanish workers who supervised the Indians. Others were put to work planting wheat, corn, and various food plants with the goal of making the mission self-sufficient. As with the other missions, the building of Mission San Diego was a slow, gradual process; years passed before all the buildings were complete. And progress was slowed because of the behavior of the soldiers in the nearby presidio, who numbered approximately fifty.

Within the first few months of arriving in San Diego, the soldiers rode into the Diegueño villages and raped the women and young girls. The Diegueño men responded with a daring daylight attack on the settlement. Spanish guns answered back, killing three natives and wounding a dozen more and embittering the Diegueño. This pattern was to be repeated with the other missions.

Serra never was able to control the soldiers and make peace with the Diegueño, let alone persuade them to help build the mission. So he used soldiers to capture Indians. Mounted on horses and armed with guns and ropes, the soldiers rode through the villages, seizing Diegueño men and women, who were marched to the site of the mission, forced to live in it, and put to work building it. This practice started in San Diego, and was followed in the early years of the other missions: forced labor and forced instruction in the Spanish way of life, along with inducements of food and clothing. One priest called the gifts of food and clothing "the bait for spiritual fishing," and he said that without these inducements, and the soldiers, the priests would have failed to build a single mission.

Two weeks after arriving in San Diego, Captain Portola, along with Father Crespi and others who were able to travel, headed north by land to establish a settlement at the harbor of Monterey, previously described by the explorer Sebastian

1. San Diego (1769)
2. San Carlos Borromeo de Carmelo (1770)
3. San Antonio de Padua (1771)
4. San Gabriel (1771)
5. San Luis Obispo (1772)
6. San Francisco (1776)
7. San Juan Capistrano (1776)
8. Santa Clara (1777)
9. San Buenaventura (1782)
10. Santa Barbara (1786)
11. La Purisima Concepcion (1787)
12. Santa Cruz (1791)
13. Soledad (1791)
14. San Jose (1797)
15. San Juan Bautista (1797)
16. San Miguel Arcángel (1797)
17. San Fernando Rey (1797)
18. San Luis Rey (1798)
19. Santa Inés (1804)
20. San Rafael (1817)
21. Solano (1823)

NEVADA

CALIFORNIA

CALIFORNIA MISSIONS

Vizcaino. When he reached Monterey, Portola didn't recognize the harbor described by Vizcaino, and no ship had arrived with food as planned. His half-starved men pushed northward along the coast until they reached San Francisco Bay on November 1, 1769. Although Father Crespi recognized the importance of the harbor, Portola didn't; he led his men back to San Diego, arriving there on January 24, 1770. Near starvation and disillusioned, the sacred expedition made plans to abandon building missions and return to Mexico. But on March 19 the *San Antonio* arrived from Mexico with food and supplies, and Serra viewed the ship's appearance as a sign from God to remain in California and establish more missions.

Leaving others in charge at San Diego, Serra headed for Monterey aboard the *San Antonio* while Portola led another party north. This time Portola recognized Monterey Bay, and with Serra, the soldiers, and the workers they established a sec ond Spanish settlement in California. Following the San Diego example, they built the presidio first so the soldiers could protect the others. Serra tried to make friends with the local Indians, the Costanoan, and he began to study their language. Shipments of food sustained the settlement; with a few dozen Indians participating, Mission San Carlos Borromeo de Carmelo, the second in California, was dedicated on June 3, 1770. It grew after soldiers marched Costanoan to the site and placed them under the control of the priests and the Spanish workers.

Over the next fifty-three years, the Spanish established nineteen more missions in California, for a total of twenty-one. Serra founded the first nine, either traveling to a suitable site with soldiers and workers, or directing another priest to do so. Besides San Diego and San Carlos Borromeo, before his death in 1784 Serra helped dedicate San Gabriel (1771), San Antonio de Padua

(1771), San Luis Obispo (1772), San Juan Capistrano (1776), San Francisco (1776), Santa Clara (1777), and San Buenaventura (1782). Serra's successor, Father Fermin Lasuen, founded the next nine: Santa Barbara (1786), La Purisima Concepcion (1787), Santa Cruz (1791), Soledad (1791), San Jose (1797), San Juan Bautista (1797), San Miguel Arcángel (1797), San Fernando Rey (1797), and San Luis Rey (1798). Santa Inés was dedicated in 1804, and San Rafael in 1817; in 1823 came Solano, the twenty-first and last mission.

The church believed that these missions would last just ten years; by then, all the natives in the area would be converted and the mission could be closed down. Instead, the missions lasted sixty-five years, from 1769 to 1834; during that time, 81,000 California Indians lived in them. With twelve-foot-high walls, with guns ever present, with brown tubes teaching them another way of life, the Diegueño and Miwok, the Esselen and Salinan, the Costanoan and Chumash encountered a strange new world unlike anything they had known. With sincerity, goodwill, and great faith, the priests tried to teach the native Californians how to be Spanish, whether they wanted to or not. For the California Indians, life in a mission meant loss of freedom, loss of dignity, loss of humanity, and loss of a culture that was 12,000 years old.

DAILY LIFE IN THE MISSIONS 5

WHETHER A CHUMASH WAS BROUGHT to Mission Santa Barbara by force, or drawn by gifts or the wish to join family and friends, once he or she entered, the door was slammed shut and it was impossible to leave. The same was true of every mission. The rules were enforced by soldiers who were always nearby; and if the Indians disobeyed, they were punished. Santa Barbara's Franciscan priests treated the Indians as their children, calling them neophytes, meaning "new converts." The priests assumed the role of parents, whose job was to teach the neophytes about reading, writing, work, morality, and God until the Indians knew God's law and could take responsibility for their own lives. The priests were responsible to God for teaching the Indians about sin and how to lead a godly life.

A day at Mission Santa Barbara, and at every mission, started at dawn with the ringing of the largest bell, the Angelus. It called the Indians to morning mass. Each Indian carried a rope to record the day's conduct: every time he or she committed a sin, such as missing mass or stealing grain from a storage bin, a knot was tied in the rope. Later, during confession, the sins were reported in the order they occurred.

Following breakfast, at the sound of another bell, it was off to the fields to tend crops and livestock, or off to the shops, where women ground corn and men made adobe bricks. The work at San Gabriel was winemaking, at San Francisco candle-making, at San Antonio the cultivation of pear trees. In a mission's early

The Presidio at Mission
San Francisco, as
depicted by Ludovik
Choris in 1816. The
stockade is in the
background; in the
foreground, mission
Indians return from
work in the fields under
the guard of a Spanish
soldier mounted on
horseback.

stages, the Indians were put to work building the mission itself. As each mission became established and produced food or other products, the surplus was used to help other missions succeed in their early years.

A bell announced lunch at eleven o'clock. Another signaled the start of the afternoon work period, when priests gave religious instruction to children. A five o'clock bell called the Indians to confession. At six a bell called them to dinner, which was followed by prayers and instruction in Spanish culture. The Poor Soul's Bell, at eight, freed the Indians to do as they pleased—so long as they committed no sins.

This was the ideal, but there never was such a day in any of the missions. Of the five hundred or so residents assembled for morning prayer in a typical mission, four hundred were women, children, teenage boys, and old men. Most of the men in their prime had escaped long ago or had died in the mission. After prayer, the Indians watched the punishment for conduct unbecoming of Christians: fifty lashes for trying to burn down the mission; seventy-five lashes for hitting a priest. Both were frequent occurrences in the missions. That done, the soldiers were dispatched to catch the previous night's runaways and rope some men in their twenties in order to put the population in balance. The Indians were then escorted to the fields and workshops by soldiers with guns.

The Franciscans kept records of daily life in the missions: food production, construction, the age of a new recruit, the age at death, what punishments were given and why. These mission records describe a world of confusion, rebellion, sickness, and starvation—and a world in which Miwok remained Miwok and Chumash stayed Chumash. Following Junipero Serra's death in 1784, Father Lasuen assumed control of the missions. In 1797, after twenty-five years of mission operation, he wrote: "The majority of our neophytes have not yet acquired much love for our way of life. Were it not for the soldiers, most of the neophytes would return to their villages."

One problem with the missions was the parent-child idea forced on the Indians. The priests called them children and treated them like children, but they were men and women, grandfathers and grandmothers, members of families, tribelets, and tribes. The priests called them children and treated them as *their* children, but they were Chumash, Esselen, Costanoan, and Miwok, not Spanish, not children of that culture. Most had been taken captive, and they were, in fact, subjects of the Spanish crown, not the children of the priests. They were confined behind the mission walls and forced into a different way of living, but they couldn't become Spanish because they were already something else. That fact alone doomed the missions to failure.

Another problem was the work requirement. No matter the mission, tribe, or year, the California Indians never adjusted to work in the missions, and for this they were severely punished. The Franciscans created a work pattern that they thought the Indians could adjust to because, they believed, it reflected Indian culture: to work at a task until it was completed instead of working for a set time. Like all the missions, Santa Barbara had a daily work allotment; women had to grind so much corn, and men had to make so many adobe bricks—360 for the Chumash brick workers. The workload was light; no Chumash was worked to death, and usually the allotment was met by noon, which provided time for more instruction, or left the worker free to do other things. Often a week's work would be done by Wednesday, leaving the worker the rest of the week off.

But after a week or a month in the mission the California

Indians, especially the men, refused to work. The problem was the *idea* of work, which was not a part of their culture. Nature told the California Indians what they should do each day, if anything; when there was nothing to do they gambled, slept, or just relaxed. There was no such thing as work for the sake of work.

Not surprisingly, the Chumash men could never understand why they had to make 360 adobe bricks when they had just made 360 the day before, and 360 the day before *that,* and the courtyard was stacked high with adobe bricks. It made no sense at all. A person who did that was about as crazy as a bird that builds a nest for the mating season and when it is finished builds another, then another, then another. The Franciscans would have failed even if they had reduced the Chumash allotment to just one brick a day. They could ring all the bells they wanted, but the Indians saw no point in doing the same thing every day for no reason at all. When the Chumash refused to work, the Franciscans saw them as lazy, and punished them. More Indians were punished for not working than for any other reason.

Another thing that went wrong was that Indians escaped from the missions, which brought more punishment. For all twenty-one missions combined, the escape rate was 10 percent, mostly young men who ran away and weren't caught. Another 30 percent tried to escape at least once but were captured by soldiers and returned to the missions. All told, 40 percent of the Indians in the missions tried to escape at least once. Sometimes they fled en masse; at Mission San Francisco in 1795, 230 Costanoan went over the wall as one. Trying to understand what they were doing wrong, the priests asked the fugitives why they ran away and recorded the answers: hunger, starvation, punishment, sickness, the death of a loved one, and "I wanted to go home."

The punishment was as confusing to the Indians as what they

were being punished for. Mission punishments were nothing like the way Indians settled disputes. They were accustomed to showing humility and not humiliating one another. But at the missions an Indian who committed a minor offense, such as missing confession, was stripped to the waist, put in stocks or held down on the ground, and given five to ten lashes by a soldier wielding a rawhide whip. Friends, family, and children were forced to watch and share in the humiliation. Justifying such punishment, Serra wrote: "We came here for the single purpose of doing them good and for their eternal salvation, and I feel that everyone knows we love them." Serra *did* truly love them. Father Lasuen wrote, "A nation which is barbarous requires more frequent punishment than a nation which is cultured." Lasuen, too, did truly love the Indians, but did believe they should be punished.

But the punishments didn't work. Mission records show that beatings were frequent and that the practice continued during the entire sixty-five-year period of the missions. Often the same Indian was whipped for the same offense over and over until he died, escaped, or just gave up.

At every turn, the neophyte broke some rule that had nothing to do with being a California Indian. Missing confession twice brought ten lashes; missing it three times or more in a week brought twenty-five. Running away, refusing to work, or praying to the Great Spirit resulted in fifty lashes, sometimes spaced over several days. A Miwok shaman at Mission San Francisco received a hundred lashes over nine days for conducting a Miwok religious ceremony. A Chumash wife watched her husband take five lashes for being late, whatever "late" was. A Chumash father watched his daughter take twenty-five for sneaking off with a boy, whatever that sin was. A Chumash grandson watched his grandfather take ten for peeling off his clothes because it was hot.

The Indians were assigned names by the priests—"Jose," "Miguel"—and a last name that reflected work—"Baker," "Carpenter." If, following Indian standards of courtesy, they didn't answer to these names or refused to speak them, they got ten lashes. To keep them from committing the sin of sleeping with young men, each night the young unmarried women were locked in a large room, the *monjerio*. If they refused to be separated from their families, they got ten lashes. The Indians were taught to say, *"Amar a Dios"*—"Love God." They already did love God, but if they didn't say the words in Spanish they got ten lashes. If a Miwok or Chumash didn't learn from the whip, food was withheld from his family. If that didn't work—if he hit a priest, killed a soldier, or tried to burn the mission down—he might be executed. Executions were rare, but each time the firing squad lined up to do its duty, the priests recorded the event. They had given the order and they had to state the reason for it, to explain to God why they had taken a human life.

The Franciscans took pride in each conversion to Christianity, even if the Indians didn't quite understand everything they were forced to believe. The California Indians learned that Christianity was a beautiful religion, rich in tradition and value but difficult to understand. They were taught that God was actually three people, the Father, Son, and Holy Ghost; that God had a son named Jesus, who came to earth; and that all people were made in God's image. But to them, the Great Spirit was present in all living things: the salmon, the oak tree, the deer, the earth itself. To the Franciscans, this view was a great sin, the sin of false worship. All 81,000 Indians who lived in the missions and were baptized into the Catholic faith were told that they were created in God's image, but that God would punish them for being who they were. To be a California Indian was a sin.

They never quite learned the lesson, according to outside observers of the missions. Visiting Mission San Francisco in 1816, the Russian artist Ludovik Choris described a Sunday service:

> All the Indians are obligated to go to church and worship. Children assist the priests with musical instruments, chiefly drums and trumpets. It is by means of this noise that they endeavor to stir the imagination of the Indians. It is, indeed, the only means of producing an effect upon them. When the drums begin to beat they fall to the ground as if they were half dead. None dares to move. All remain stretched upon the ground without making the slightest movement until the end of the service and, even then, it is necessary to tell them several times that the mass is finished. Armed soldiers are stationed at each corner of the church.

Ten years later the British scientist Frederick Beechey described a Sunday service in the same mission:

> The congregation was arranged on both sides of the building, separated by a wide aisle passing along the center in which were stationed several bailiffs with whips, canes, and goads to preserve silence and maintain order, and what seemed more difficult than either, to keep the congregation in their kneeling posture. The goads were better adapted to this purpose than the whips, as they would reach a long way and inflict a sharp puncture without making any noise. The end of the church was occupied by soldiers under arms with fixed bayonets.

ESTANISLAO'S CHOICE 6

HILE THE CHUMASH AND OTHERS were answering bells on the coast, the interior tribes still had the freedom to live in their natural world. There were no missions in the San Joaquin Valley, because the Spanish had learned not to build them in remote areas where they were hard to defend. In 1680 Pueblo Indians in New Mexico began a general revolt and were joined by Hopi, Navajo, and Apache. Four hundred Spaniards were killed, including twenty-one of the thirty-three missionaries. In 1704, a thousand Creek warriors—backed by the English, who wanted land held by Spain—drove the Spanish out of northeast Florida, burning three priests at the stake. As a result, the missions of California were built near the coast and spaced one day's travel apart so soldiers from one mission could ride to defend another. Racing up and down El Camino Real, the road linking the missions, the soldiers were to shoot Indians who attacked the missions.

Without guns, horses, or armor, the coastal tribes fought to preserve their way of life, and El Camino Real became a highway of death. After repeated attacks, Mission San Diego was moved six miles inland to the home of another Diegueño tribelet. In 1775, eight hundred Diegueño burned the mission down and captured its priest, Father Luis Jayme, as he shouted, *"¡Amar a Dios, hijos!"*—"Love God, my children!" He was clubbed to death and shot with eighteen arrows.

A Spanish soldier on
horseback confronts Indians
armed with bows and
arrows while Indian women
look on from the doorway
of a domed thatch house.
Made during the 1791
Malaspina expedition from
Spain, it is believed to be
the earliest image of
fighting between the
Spanish and Indians in
California.

At news of the disaster, Serra rejoiced, "Thanks be to God. Now that the terrain has been watered by blood, the conversion of the San Diego Indians will take place." More soldiers were moved to the area, and new recruits were marched to the mission site. The mission was rebuilt—and, as at other missions that had been set on fire or would be in the future, the new buildings featured roofs of adobe tile instead of the old flammable wood and straw.

Despite Serra's hopes, Mission San Diego was attacked again in 1778. Some Christian Indians who had escaped from the mission participated in the attack and were captured by the Spanish. They were given fifty lashes each; one died from the punishment. During Serra's years in California, hardly a month passed without his writing to authorities in Mexico requesting more soldiers and guns to defend the missions. The same was true for his successor, Father Lasuen.

The day after Mission San Gabriel started in 1771 Gabrieleno attacked the guard: a soldier had raped the wife of their chief. They were beaten back; the chief was killed and his head was mounted on a pole at the site of the mission as a lesson to other Indians. In 1785 a Gabrieleno woman named Toypurina led six tribelets against the mission, but the warriors were outmatched by Spanish rifles and cannons. In 1824 the Chumash in Mission Santa Barbara burned the mission to the ground and fled to the hills. In the same year 2,000 other Chumash battered La Purisima for three months. Warfare raged at Santa Clara and San Juan Bautista in the 1790s, and in 1793 Francisco Palou, the head priest at Mission San Francisco, lamented: "No journey is possible without a military escort, even between one mission and its neighboring mission. In traveling from one to the other, we are constantly under the attack of pagans who occupy the territory in between."

Having escaped from Mission San Jose as a young man, the rebel Estanislao led a force of Miwok against the Spanish until the soldiers trapped his band in a forest and set the trees on fire. Estanislao's men were cut down as they tried to escape, and he was ordered to surrender. He shouted that his people preferred "the quick death of a bullet to the slow death of civilization." The soldiers complied, shooting the survivors as they ran from the flames and killing all but three women.

No mission escaped Indian attack and no priest was entirely safe. The first three priests at San Miguel were poisoned to death, as was San Antonio's priest. When Indians at Santa Cruz poisoned Father Andres Quintana, they were so clever that the death was not revealed as a murder for two years. Whether in or outside the missions, the coastal tribes wanted just one thing: to be left alone. When their land was seized, when their mothers, daughters, fathers, and sons were kidnapped and held against their will, they did not think it savage to fight back. A leader of the Diegueño was captured and asked why his people wanted to kill all the priests and soldiers. He answered for the coastal tribes: "In order to live as we did before."

When it became clear that that was impossible, the coastal tribes fled to the interior. Had they known what awaited them there, they might have preferred Estanislao's choice and taken a bullet instead. They were no better off in the valleys and mountains than the people they knew in the missions. The slow death of civilization had spread to every corner of the state, and the San Joaquin Valley had become a valley of death.

Like other Native Americans, California Indians had no resistance to European diseases; they cut the Indians down like a terrible swift sword. Tuberculosis killed half the Ohlone in and around Mission Santa Clara in 1777 before it spread to the interior of the state and killed Indians living there. Pneumonia and diphtheria epidemics ravaged San Carlos Borromeo, Soledad, San Antonio, San Miguel, San Luis Obispo, and La Purisima, and were carried to the San Joaquin Valley by runaways. In 1806 measles swept through every mission from San Diego to San Francisco, killing 1,600 people, including nearly all children under ten years of age. Measles hit again in 1827, and again spread to all twenty-one missions. More than half of all Indian children born in the missions died before reaching their fifth birthday. In every mission deaths exceeded births by a wide margin, and more than a third of all babies were born dead—and these figures don't include those who were purposely killed by their parents as a protest against the missions. To care for the sick and dying, the Franciscans brought one doctor for all of California.

The missions made these diseases deadlier than they might have been. Once, the Indians had been healthy on a diet of meat, fish, acorns, and seeds; in the missions they ate a starchy mush of barley soup for breakfast, lunch, and dinner. One of their most frequent complaints was that they were starving to death; and their condition worsened when they refused to work or otherwise disobeyed and food was withheld from their families. The Miwok in San Francisco were given drinking water from the same stream in which human waste was dumped. The Chumash in Santa Barbara were infected by rats that lived in the permanent adobe buildings where they were housed. They could neither leave the mission to gather plants that they knew cured some ailments, nor could they burn their village and resettle elsewhere. During the history of Mission Santa Barbara, from 1786 to 1834, 4,771 Chumash were converted to the Catholic faith. During the same period, 4,645 Chumash were buried in the mission graveyard. Of this number, only thirty had been ill when they entered the mission.

Death by starvation, death by disease, death by punishment, and death by war did not end the misery of all captives. For women and young girls there was also death from rape. Soldiers came with the missions, and when they raped, they spread syphilis, a deadly sexually transmitted disease for which there was then no cure. The priests couldn't stop the rapes—they couldn't send the soldiers away without being killed themselves. Jose Benites, the only doctor in California, reported in 1804 that measles was the most devastating disease and syphilis was second. In 1817 the priest at San Francisco reported that nearly all the mission women were so weak from syphilis they could not work. Syphilis killed them directly, or weakened their resistance to other diseases, or caused their babies to be born dead. When a baby was born alive and the father was clearly Spanish, the baby was often strangled by the mother—and she then took a hundred lashes for the mortal sin.

As they recorded such events, it occurred to some priests that things weren't going as planned. The workshops were stocked with Christian Indians—but so was the graveyard. The priests' complaints to Father Serra, and later to Father Lasuen, were full of anguish. "I am weary of all this sickness and dying," Father Narcisco Duran wrote in 1802 in the death register he kept at Mission San Jose. "There are many deaths and few births," Father Jose Viader wrote in 1830 at Santa Clara. "Sickness is always with us, and I fear it is the end of the Indian race. What can we do?" Before he was clubbed to death, Father Jayme of Mission San Diego complained of soldiers who made a sport of roping and raping Indian women: "Many times the natives have come here to kill us all because soldiers went into their villages and raped their women. . . . I feel very deeply about the fact that what the devil does not accomplish among the pagans, Christians will accomplish."

Some priests asked to be transferred to a monastery where they could live the rest of their lives in solitude. Some fled after just a few months of service. Conditions at Soledad were so depressing that thirty priests passed through there during its early years. Determined to stop the baby-killing at San Gabriel, Father Jose Zalvidea punished one woman by having her head shaved, having her whipped daily for fifteen days, having her feet bound in irons for three months, and having her appear every Sunday in church at the altar with a hideously painted wooden child in her arms. He suffered a nervous breakdown and was relieved of duty. In 1799, after just a few months of service at San Miguel, Father Antonio Horra was so enraged he wrote to civil authorities in Mexico: "The treatment shown to Indians is the most cruel I have ever seen in history. For the slightest things they receive heavy flogging, are shackled, and put in the stocks, and treated with so much cruelty that they are kept whole days without a drink of water." The Franciscan Order in California intercepted Horra's letter. He was isolated, examined, declared insane, and taken out of California under armed guard.

But complaints about the missions continued to mount. Having visited some missions in 1786, a French nobleman observed that the mission Indian was "sullen, listless and dull," while the Russian artist Ludovik Choris said he never saw an Indian laugh in a mission and added, "They look as though they are interested in nothing." Another Russian in California, the otter hunter Vassilli Tarakanoff, visited Mission Santa Barbara in the 1820s and described a group of Chumash who were being returned to the mission:

> They were all bound with rawhide ropes and some were bleeding from wounds and some children were tied to their mothers. Some of the run-away men were tied on sticks and beaten with straps. One chief was taken out to the open field and a young calf that had just died was skinned and the chief was sewed into the skin while it was yet warm. He was kept tied to a stake all day, but he died soon and they kept his corpse tied up.

In the 1820s and 1830s civil authorities—governors and mayors—in Mexico and California began calling for an end to the missions through "secularization." Under secularization, the missions would be operated by "secular" clergymen, who did not belong to a monastic order, and the Indians would be free to leave. Among the advocates of secularization were the greedy and self-serving, who cared little about the mission Indians. By the 1830s the missions possessed much of California's wealth: stockpiles of wheat, vast herds of cattle, and sprawling orchards of apples, pears, plums, and grapes. It has been estimated that by 1832 the twenty-one missions owned a total of 308,121 cattle, sheep, goats, pigs, horses, and mules, and a total of 12,070 tons of wheat, barley, corn, beans, peas, and other plant foods. People who had no stake in the missions wanted them turned over to a secular clergy, and wanted the missions' wealth offered for sale or transferred to the civilian residents of California.

Others clamoring for the end of the missions had a genuine concern for the Indians. They were influenced by the intellectual movement called the Enlightenment, which started in the eighteenth century. An important Enlightenment idea was that every person has the right to freedom. This belief helped bring about the American Revolution, led the European nations to abolish slavery, and was influential in Mexico's declaration of independence from Spain. Mexico won its independence in 1821, gaining control of California, and Mexican revolutionaries came to view the missions as a form of slavery. Besides, most of the missionaries had been born in Spain and considered themselves superior to people born in Mexico—namely, the Mexican revolutionaries. So they were natural targets for the revolutionary government.

In August 1833 the Mexican congress passed a law providing for secularization, which was to be conducted over the next two years. The Mexican governor of California, Jose Figueroa, appointed twenty-one administrators, one for each mission, and sent them to assume control. Seeing the end, some priests slaughtered their cattle and sold the hides to salvage as much wealth as possible for the church. As a consequence, when the administrators arrived, they found the missions surrounded by thousands of skinned carcasses rotting in the sun. By Figueroa's proclamation of August 9, 1834, which modified the earlier law, half of all mission property was to go to the Indians, who by law were forbidden to dispose of it. As secularization proceeded, it wasn't clear how much land the Indians would actually receive, but by 1834 one thing was clear: most of the Indians in the missions had died before they ever had a chance to become Spanish or receive mission land.

During the mission period, from 1769 to 1834, the population of the coastal tribes fell from 72,000 to 18,000, a decline of 75 percent. When the missions started, there were around 400,000 California Indians. Sixty-five years later, 150,000 were left. One of them, still alive and still living in a mission in 1834, said, "I am very old. My people were once around me like the sands of the shore . . . many . . . many. They have all passed away. They have died like the grass. . . . I am all that is left of my people. I am alone."

PART III
THE GOLD RUSH

Kintpuash—known by whites as "Captain Jack"—in a photograph taken after his capture by the U.S. Army. A Modoc chief, Kintpuash led the last significant revolt by California Indians against white settlement. (*See Chapter 9.*)

Grass Valley, Nevada County, California, 1852. This print shows the impact of white settlement on the California landscape: land enclosed for cultivation and livestock, timber being cut for the sawmill (right foreground), and farms and buildings springing up beneath the flag of the United States. In the left foreground, two miners with picks and pans rest under a tree.

THE ARRIVAL OF THE AMERICANS 7

IN 1797 FATHER LASUEN had observed that the Indians in the missions weren't becoming Spanish and that only force kept them in the missions. In 1834 these facts had not changed. At the time of secularization, there were about 15,000 Indians still living in the missions. When the doors were unlocked and they were free to choose, approximately 10,000 of them tried to return home. But home was gone. Where there had once been a village with areas for dancing and trading, now there was only an open space, with ground that had been scarred by galloping horses. Most of the 10,000 drifted into the San Joaquin Valley, where European diseases continued to spread death.

Perhaps 2,000 of the 5,000 who stayed behind continued living in the missions. The missions hadn't closed, and because there was no secular clergy in California to replace the Franciscan priests, the Franciscans still conducted mass and heard confessions. The Indians who remained in the missions tended small gardens, served as cooks, and assisted the priests at mass. Though they were free to leave, they never did. Their tribes had also been destroyed, and the missions still produced some food and offered living quarters.

The remaining 3,000 who stayed behind on the coast lived near the missions but didn't join the other coastal Indians, who were still living as they always had. The former mission Indians didn't know the coastal people and no longer remembered the particulars of the World Renewal Ceremony or the point of

Coyote disregarding the rules in nature. They weren't Chumash and Miwok anymore, but they weren't Spanish either. They had lost their culture, lost their identity, and lost their purpose in life. They were like the African Americans who after 250 years of slavery and the loss of their culture were suddenly freed and told to be somebody.

The Indians who survived the missions were citizens of the Republic of Mexico, but they weren't Mexican, and they weren't any better off under a new ruler. During secularization, thousands of colonists from Mexico traveled north to California with the aim of acquiring some of the missions' wealth. Conflict developed between the colonists and the twenty-one administrators appointed by Governor Figueroa. The colonists charged the administrators with being too slow in assessing the value of crops, livestock, and mission land, and too slow in offering this wealth for sale.

Impatient, the colonists simply overran some missions, looted their warehouses, stole the remaining livestock, and seized mission land. Some of the soldiers who once had guarded the priests took part in the thievery. Through bribery and the promise of future favors, government officials and high-ranking citizens secured large grants of land and agricultural products at a fraction of their value, or as a gift. Overnight, they became the richest men in the state. They built huge farms and ranches and started many of California's industries: wine, cattle, and fruit and vegetable growing.

The Franciscan priests and some of Figueroa's administrators fought to see that the governor's order was carried out: half of all mission land was supposed to go to the Indians, who weren't allowed to sell it. No one knows how many acres the Indians actually received, but it was certainly less than a tenth of the mission land, and by 1836 Figueroa's proclamation was changed to allow the Indians to sell their parcels.

For a time, some Indians tried to make a living by farming their land near the mission buildings, but none managed to keep their allotments for more than a few years. Their land was seized and added to farms and ranches. Some Indians traded their land for liquor, and stayed drunk as long as they could. They wore Mexican clothes and spoke a mixture of Spanish and Indian languages; they wandered around in a haze without a purpose in life. Alcohol was new to them; when they stumbled and fell, Mexicans laughed at the sight of the ever-present drunken Indian.

They drifted into the growing towns of Los Angeles, San Diego, Santa Barbara, and San Jose, where they found work as day laborers, laying brick and doing odd jobs. They were paid in cheap whiskey and rum, not in cash, and this kept them coming back, assuring employers a steady supply of cheap labor. Los Angeles was so dependent on Indian labor that once a week it auctioned off Indian jail inmates to those who needed workers. The Indians drank up their weekly earnings, were thrown in jail for drunkenness, and on Sunday were auctioned off again.

Another 4,000 Indians, including some who had never been missionized, worked on farms and ranches where they were paid in food, clothing, and alcohol. They slept in the fields with their bottles until a bell announced the start of the workday.

The Mexican Army in California sometimes marched to the San Joaquin Valley to kill Miwok and Yokuts for raiding and stealing, but Mexico's rule of California was brief and mostly peaceful. While it held the state, from 1822 to 1848, few natives either knew their land had changed hands or had any contact with the new owners. Disease continued to kill some. The Yurok, Hupa, and Tolowa declined when the Russian colony at Fort Ross wiped out their food supply. The Russians killed nearly all the seals, sea lions, and otters along the northern coast; in 1842, with nothing left to hunt, they pulled out. They sold the fort and everything in it to the American John Sutter, who operated a large farm and cattle ranch in the Sacramento Valley using Indian labor. Four years later, a visitor to Sutter's ranch described what went on there, and it was a sign of bad things to come. The traveler said that Sutter kept 600 to 800 Indians "in a complete state of slavery." He fed them in four-foot-long troughs where they scooped food out with their hands and ate "like so many pigs."

A new chapter in the life of the California Indians began in the 1830s and 1840s with the arrival of Americans. While hunting in the mountains in the eastern part of the state, men of the Modoc, Yana, and Yahi began encountering burly men dressed in animal fur who drew rifles at the sight of an Indian. Without asking anyone, Mexicans or Indians, the American mountain men laid traps and shot deer and elk to meet the demand on the East Coast for hide and fur. By the time they had penetrated the interior of the state in the early 1840s, their country had reduced its own Indian population by half.

In the 1830s the President of the United States, Andrew Jackson, was removing all Indians who lived east of the Mississippi River and forcing them to live in a barren land called the Indian Territory in Oklahoma. The way to Oklahoma was called the Trail of Tears because of the thousands of Indians who died en route. Jackson called Native Americans "savages" and "barbarians"; he had spent most of his life fighting them. So had the mountain men moving into Wyoming, Idaho, Oregon, and California.

The mountain men shared President Jackson's view that the Indians were uncivilized. But unlike the Spanish, the Americans had no wish to civilize them—they only wanted to take their land, and shoot them if they resisted. And America was one of the few countries that still had human slavery. Hiding behind trees, the Yahi watched from a great distance as the long beards set traps on the banks of the Feather River. Contact with them might mean death.

At the same time, American merchants and traders, like Sutter, established businesses in Mexican California, put Indians to work, and drove off those who wouldn't work; they had no wish to civilize Indians either. What these merchants wanted more than anything else was American control of California. In particular, they wanted control of the port of San Francisco, which in turn would give them control of the lucrative trade between North America and the Far East. Competition for the China trade, as it was known, was the main cause of the war that started between the United States and Mexico in 1846. Mexico lost and in 1848 ceded California, Texas, and the Southwest to the United States. Once again, California changed hands by war, but most California Indians weren't aware of it.

In a humane move, Mexico tried to ensure that the Indians would be allowed to live as Indians under American rule. Mexico had abolished slavery in 1830—the United States wouldn't do so for another thirty-five years—and Mexico knew how the new rulers of California treated Native Americans. By the 1848 Treaty of Guadalupe Hidalgo, which ended the war, Mexico secured an agreement from the United States specifying that when land claims were being settled in California the Indians should be given preference and allowed to keep their land. Article XI of the treaty bound the United States to observe that "special care shall . . . be taken not to place its Indian occupants under the necessity of seeking new homes." There was little chance the United States would honor the treaty. It had already signed 300 treaties with Native Americans and broken nearly every one. When President

Jackson removed the eastern Indians to Oklahoma, he broke more than a hundred treaties at once.

The ink had hardly dried on the peace treaty when news spread that gold had been discovered in northern California, triggering the California gold rush of 1849. This was the most important event in all of California's history so far. From every part of America, hundreds of thousands of gold-seekers poured into the newly acquired territory. Excluding the Indians, in 1845 California's population was only about 7,000. Six months after gold was discovered, California had enough people to qualify for statehood, 60,000, and in 1850 it became the thirty-first state, with a population of more than 150,000.

San Francisco captured the China trade, and by the time the rush ended in 1860 the gold reserves of the United States were piled high as a mountain and thousands of Californians were rich. Between 1848 and 1860 the state produced $600 million worth of gold. Between 1848 and 1860 the state's population increased from 20,000 to more than 300,000. By 1860 California, not Washington or Oregon, dominated the West Coast. By 1860 California was so important that plans were made to build a transcontinental railroad to link it to the rest of the nation.

In stories written about the thrilling California gold rush, crusty old prospectors on mules struck it rich, then lost the fortune in a game of poker. Easterners read these "dime novels" and felt the excitement of gold rush California. Caravans of huge wagons rolled through deserts and mountains carrying merchants, bankers, gold-seekers, and outlaws. When ships docked in San Francisco, their passengers scurried down planks and raced to the gold fields, stopping only long enough to buy a pick, a pan, and a map. There were footraces down the city's muddy streets. There were barroom brawls and shootouts. In the mining regions of the Sierra Nevada foothills there was adventure in every pan of silt scooped from the stream. Sitting around campfires late at night, the prospectors told colorful tales about luck and misfortune, about home and families left behind, and about savage Indians who were killed for getting in the way. By 1860 the gold reserves were piled high as a mountain—and so were the bodies of the Miwok, Chumash, Yana, and Yahi.

This 1849 photograph of miners at the gold rush diggings at Taylorsville includes several Indians among the whites. Many Indians worked the mines, although few profited by it and most worked for white miners in conditions of near-slavery.

"GOOD HAUL OF DIGGERS" 8

URING THE 1850s, the California Indians didn't know they were participating in the color and excitement of the gold rush decade. They were too busy fighting for their lives. America—whatever "America" was—had laid claim to their land. The forty-niners arrived, swamped the valleys and streams, and the "gold rush" was on—whatever that was. Americans believed in "Manifest Destiny," the idea that it was God's plan to expand America from the East to the West Coast, but the California Indians hadn't heard it. They hadn't signed any treaty giving up their land. They hadn't issued invitations to have their home destroyed. And as far as they knew, they hadn't done anything to deserve being driven from their homes.

The forty-niners had a different view. The forty-niners had read about the savages out west, and they brought to California a certain image of what the Indian was like: naked, dirty, wild, and bloodthirsty. He was forever wandering about, with no real home and no claim to the land. He didn't farm, he didn't have a written language, and with no knowledge of morality he was a thief, a liar, and a cheat. A godless heathen forever bent on war, he raped white women and scalped white men. Uncivilized and subhuman, he was seen as a natural obstacle to be overcome, like a dangerous river or a steep mountain pass. As President Andrew Jackson said in 1830: "What good man would prefer a country covered with forests and ranged by a few thousand savages to our extensive Republic

. . . with all the blessings of liberty, civilization, and religion?"

As fast as a rifle's bullet, the image of the "Digger" Indian was created so he could be killed or driven away. The *San Francisco Chronicle,* one of the state's leading newspapers, said the California Indians "grazed in the fields like beasts and ate roots, snakes, and grasses like cattle, like pigs, like dogs . . . and like hungry wolves." One forty-niner said they slept "like animals in a pigsty." Another likened them to reptiles, saying they were "coiled up like a parcel of snakes." When he encountered some Maidu in 1850, a miner from Connecticut exclaimed, "What heathens they are!" Referring to Modoc in 1853, a Humboldt County newspaper declared, "We can never rest in security until the red skins are treated like the other wild beasts of the forest." As early as April 1849, the newspaper *Alta California* predicted that in order for whites to mine gold "it will be absolutely necessary to exterminate the savages."

The war against the California Indians started when the first forty-niners rushed in. Early in 1849 white miners from Oregon entered a Maidu village, raped several women, and shot the men who tried to resist. When the Maidu killed five of the Oregon men in retaliation, the Oregon miners struck back by attacking the village, killing a dozen Indians and executing seven more afterward. During the summer of 1849 other miners from parts unknown attacked a Southern Maidu village, killing thirty natives and wounding ten more, who were then knifed to death. In August five miners disappeared from a camp in the land of the Wintun; although there was no proof that Indians were involved, the miners formed a posse and attacked a Wintun tribelet. They killed twenty and captured eighty; when the captives tried to escape, all eighty were shot to death.

In 1849 the Pomo killed two white ranchers for raping Pomo

women and mistreating Indian workers. To stop future attacks by the Pomo, in May 1850 the U.S. Army was dispatched to the home of the Pomo at Clear Lake. The Pomo met the army in peace, but the soldiers attacked, killing 135 men, women, and children. Captain N. Lyon, who led the troops, ordered his men to encircle the Pomo village and move in firing their rifles. He described the result as "a perfect slaughter pen." The Pomo fell, one observer said, "as grass before the sweep of the scythe." This was the gold rush as it was known to California Indians, and it was just getting started.

In 1850 it hit them like a tidal wave. Whites overran their land by the thousands, and during the 1850s and 1860s the Indians were swept away like unwanted debris. Red Bluff, Marysville, and other towns offered bounties for Indian scalps, arms, and hands, or other proof of a dead Indian; there was no discussion of whether a severed limb had belonged to a peaceful or hostile Indian. Whites formed unofficial militia units to kill Indians and submitted claims for expenses to the state. In 1851 and 1852 the state paid $1 million in such claims, and in 1857 issued $400,000 in bonds to pay the expenses of volunteers engaged in "the suppression of Indian hostilities."

Governor John McDougall in 1850 and Governor Peter Burnett in 1851 endorsed a war of extermination against California Indians, and local newspapers carried stories of men who hunted and shot Indians for sport. The *Humboldt Times* ran bold headlines: "Good Haul of Diggers—Band Exterminated" and "Good Haul of Diggers—Thirty-eight Bucks Killed, Forty Squaws and Children Taken." In March 1859 when a white raiding party in Humboldt killed Yurok men and captured the women and children, the *Times* reported what happened to the captives as casually as if reporting the slaughter of cattle: "All the squaws were killed because they refused to go further. The infants were put out of their misery, and a girl ten years of age was killed for stubbornness."

These dead Yurok were a drop in the bucket compared to others who died in the massacres of the 1850s. Besides the Clear Lake Massacre, white miners and ranchers killed 150 Modoc on the south fork of the Trinity River in 1852, after one of their number was accused of killing a white miner. Reporting on the Trinity River killings, Indian agent Redick McKee wrote, "In all the frontier settlements of California, there are many men who value the life of an Indian just as they do that of a coyote, or a wolf, and embrace every occasion to shoot them down." In 1853, 450 Tolowa were massacred near the Smith River in the northeastern corner of California; the babies who survived the massacre were tied to weights and thrown into the river. Referring to the Smith River killings, a government investigator lamented, "Squatters evidently think that an Indian has no rights that a white man is bound to respect. They think that all should be killed off, and not infrequently they boast of the number of 'bucks' they have killed, as if it were an achievement to be proud of."

On February 26, 1860, Wiyot living on an island in Humboldt Bay were attacked, a local newspaper said, because whites were annoyed by the chanting and dancing of the Wiyot World Renewal Ceremony. Whites living in the region rowed across the bay to the island and killed 188 men, women, and children. In his official report of the massacre, Major Gabriel Raines, the commander at Fort Humboldt, wrote, "I have just been to Indian Island, the home of a band of friendly Indians, where I beheld a scene of atrocity and horror unparalleled not only in our own country, but even in history—babies with brains oozing out of their skulls, cut and hacked with axes, a two year old child with its ear and scalp torn from the side of its little head, and squaws exhibiting the most frightful wounds, their heads split in twain by axes." Describing another massacre in 1858, also in Humboldt, government investigator John Ross Browne wrote, "Girls and boys lay here and there with their throats cut from ear to ear; men and women clinging to each other in terror were found perforated with bullets or cut to pieces with knives— all were cruelly murdered."

For others, death was more silent, more gradual. The Yurok found their salmon streams polluted with silt from the digging for gold. The Yahi discovered that the oyster beds they relied on at the mouth of the Sacramento River were ruined by pollution. When trees were cut down to build settlements, the deer and elk that the Modoc needed to live disappeared. Hydraulic mining, by which hillsides were sprayed with large quantities of water, destroyed plants and wildlife habitats; now the Modoc could no longer gather berries when deer were scarce. Farms sprang up and valuable hunting and gathering lands were lost. Oak trees were felled for pastures, while farmers fed the acorns to their hogs. The gold rush meant death by starvation for thousands of Indians, and death from disease for thousands more.

Others died when they fought to avoid enslavement. Rushed through the first state legislature in 1850, the Indian Indenture Act made it legal to own Indians and to work them as slaves. According to the law, if a miner saw an Indian in a public place— sitting on a bench in front of a hardware store, for example—and if the Indian seemed to be loitering and a nuisance—talking loudly and not working but whittling a stick—then the white miner could have the Indian arrested for vagrancy. A white judge heard the case, and if the Indian was declared to be a vagrant, a fine was imposed and within twenty-four hours the Indian was auctioned to the highest bidder. The Indian had to work for the miner, rancher, or farmer until the fine was paid off, perhaps three months. But owners of Indians often ignored the law; the average length of labor under the Indian Indenture Act was fifteen to twenty years, with no guarantee of payment for work. Before the law was repealed in 1863, about 10,000 Indians had been sold and forced to work mining gold, tending crops, and herding cattle.

For those who weren't sold under the law, the Indian Indenture Act opened up another kind of slavery. Once it was legal to own Indians, whites kidnapped Indian women and children and abused them sexually or sold them for that purpose to other forty-niners. Here was how the law worked for many Indian tribelets: suddenly a village was besieged by white slave raiders; the Indian men were shot and the women and children captured. This was why warfare raged throughout the state for its first twenty years. This was why Yana men took bullets to the chest and why Yokuts men were decapitated. They weren't fighting merely to retain a way of life, to keep their streams clean and their oak groves standing. They were fighting against the greatest horror of all: the loss of their wives and children before their very eyes.

The practice of kidnapping Indian women and children was widespread and not hidden. In December 1861, the *Marysville Appeal* reported the activity, stating that children were seized as servants while young women were captured for "the purpose of labor and lust." Settlers wouldn't pay more than $60 for a boy, the *Appeal* noted, but willingly paid $100 or more for "a likely young girl." A forty-niner in Eureka observed, "It is a common practice in this country to buy and sell Digger Indians, especially young females who bring from twenty to forty dollars each."

The *Ukiah Mendocino Herald* reported prices of $50 to $200 for children from six to fifteen, noting that girls brought the highest price, while in Humboldt County a forty-niner traded his horse "for a good little Digger."

As part of a long letter to an army friend, Colonel Francis Lippitt of Fort Humboldt paused to discuss the subject: "Individuals and parties are constantly engaged in kidnapping Indian children, frequently attacking the ranches, and killing the parents for no other purpose. This is said to be a very lucrative business, the kidnapped children bringing good prices, in some instances . . . hundreds of dollars apiece." One slave raider in Trinity County made $15,000 in six months by capturing and selling 400 women and children. No one knows the exact numbers, but it has been estimated that at least 5,000 children were kidnapped and sold, and another 5,000 women and young girls were kidnapped and sold.

Trying to save them, their fathers, brothers, and sons fell to the ground in equal numbers, but the slave raiders kept coming. The salmon were gone, the oak trees destroyed, and there was nowhere to go that was beyond the reach of the forty-niners. "In all those districts where white men are numerous," the *San Francisco Alta California* accurately reported in 1859, "the Indians have been killed off; many tribes have entirely disappeared." In 1769 there were 400,000 California Indians; in 1834, 150,000; in 1848, 125,000; in 1855, 65,000; in 1860, 35,000.

Government agents and
representatives of northern
California Indian tribes meet to
establish the Round Valley
reservation, 1858. As elsewhere
in California, establishment of a
reservation did little to protect
Indians from the onslaught of
white settlers: Squatters forced
Indians off the land, often with
the cooperation of the Indian
agents assigned to protect them,
and by the mid-1860s four-fifths
of the reservation had been lost
to whites.

KINTPUASH'S CHOICE 9

HE MODOC FELL without knowing the Yurok were dying. The Chumash were shot without knowing the Miwok were starving. The mountain of corpses that grew during the gold rush made the experience of California Indians resemble that of other Native Americans. When Europeans arrived in North America, 10 million people were living there. By 1910, only 230,000 Native Americans were left.

On average during the gold rush decade, 6,500 California Indians died each year, 540 each month, eighteen each day— almost one every hour from 1849 to 1860. The Yurok fought and retreated to another river, where they prayed for the return of the salmon. To escape the slave raiders, the Chumash moved to a distant oak grove whose previous owners were nowhere to be found. Now living in tribelets of fifty or twenty-five, the men of the Modoc climbed mountains 10,000 feet high to hunt deer, elk, or whatever else had fled the gold rush by moving higher. They knew they were dying out, and their only chance for survival was to retreat to find a new food supply and shelter. The fish, the deer, the oak—the land, was their life. It gave them culture and purpose. If they lost the land, they were nothing.

In 1849, even before California became a state, even before forty-niners staked claims to Indian land, Territorial Governor Richard Mason said that California Indians had no right to any land in California. The majority of whites agreed. At the start of the wars of extermination in the 1850s, Governor John Bigler urged that the U.S. Army move against the Indians and drive them out of California. Addressing the legislature in 1851, Governor Peter Burnett said, "That a war of extermination will continue to be waged between the two races until the Indian race becomes extinct must be expected." The majority of whites agreed. They were killing Indians and driving them off their land when they encountered two obstacles, obstacles that meant there was a chance Indians might be allowed to live and keep some of their land.

The first was a federal law, passed in 1793, under which Indian land could be acquired only by treaty, and only the federal government could negotiate and sign those treaties. The second obstacle was Article XI of the 1848 treaty that ended the war with Mexico. By this provision the United States had pledged that it would take "special care" to allow Indians to live on their ancestral lands. In other words, the state of California could not simply take Indian land. Only the federal government could sign treaties with Indians, and Indians had to agree to give up their land.

While the army, state militia, bounty hunters, and slave raiders moved against the Indians, three federal negotiators traveled throughout the state in 1851 and 1852 to establish peace and sign treaties with Indians—against the will of most white Californians. Traveling under armed guard, Redick McKee, George Barbour, and Dr. Oliver Wozencraft met with 402 chiefs and signed eighteen treaties. Some of the treaties were dictated, forced upon tribes too weak to resist. Some tribes signed in the hope of stopping the kidnapping and bloodshed. By the eighteen treaties the Indians surrendered their aboriginal claim to California. (An aboriginal claim is one based on being in a place first.) In return, they were granted 7.4 million acres of land, where they could live as Indians under the protection of the U.S. government. The alternative was more starvation, kidnapping, and death. However unfair it was to be forced into giving up a home occupied for 12,000 years to newcomers, at least the California Indians had been promised permanent title to some land.

But California's lawmakers opposed granting any land to the Indians. In 1851 the state legislature met and denounced the eighteen treaties. Both the assembly and the senate drafted reports instructing the state's U.S. representatives and senators to stop ratification of the treaties by the U.S. Senate. Expressing their desire that there be no Indian land, the California legislators passed a resolution insisting that the California Indians be removed "beyond the limits of the State in which they are found with all practicable dispatch." At the same time the lawmakers were careful to distinguish between "wild" or "hostile" Indians, who should be removed, and those called "tame" and "useful," who should be allowed to stay. In the latter category were Indians who worked for white farmers and ranchers: this important source of cheap labor was "useful" to whites.

The eighteen treaties were submitted to the U.S. Senate for approval on June 1, 1852. California's congressmen and senators pulled strings and promised favors, and on July 7, in a secret session, the treaties were rejected and declared classified; they remained a secret until Indians discovered them and made them public in 1905. Meanwhile, the gold rush continued until there were hardly any Indians left to lay claim to land.

In 1853, Congress passed a law granting the California Indians five reservations of 25,000 acres each—far less than they had been promised under the eighteen treaties. The Hoopa Valley reservation in Humboldt County, Round Valley in Mendocino, Nome Lackee in Sacramento, Tule River in Tulare, and Tejon in Kern County were the first reservations in the nation and were created on the advice of Edward Beale, the new superintendent of Indian affairs for California. It was Beale's desire that the Indians live on the reservations, where they would be taught farming and handicrafts, much in the manner of the Spanish missions but without religious instruction. Beale hoped that the Indians would ultimately become self-sufficient, just as the Franciscan priests had planned.

Starting in late 1853, the army was dispatched, and the Shasta, the Modoc, and the others who hadn't died yet were asked to abandon oak groves and hunting grounds and live on the reservations. The tribelets too weak to fight complied. The tribelets strong enough to fight resisted. They had earlier signed a treaty granting them far more land, and they wanted the whites to live up to that agreement. But it did them no good when their chiefs waved the treaties and reminded the whites of the earlier commitment. Now that the reservations had been created, white militia companies were bent on clearing Indians off their land or burying them in it, whichever was easier. To many whites, if not most, there was little difference between concentrating Indians on a distant reservation and exterminating them.

Operating in Shasta and Trinity counties, a unit called the Kibble Guards "collected" Indians, one member recalled, for the reservation. He said they located Indian camps, surrounded them at night, attacked them at dawn, then marched the survivors to the reservation. Another unit, Jarboe's Rangers, boasted that in less than four months it had killed 283 Indians and delivered 292 to the reservation. Praising the work of the Rangers, a settler wrote to the *Sonoma Journal* in 1859: "To persons seeking good ranches . . . as soon as the Indian difficulties are disposed of, you will find satisfactory locations in this region."

In Butte County the Indians were given thirty days to leave or be killed. "Indians! Indians!" the editor of the *Butte County Appeal* screamed in one column. "We call upon the citizens of the county to aid in the removal of these festering devils." In Fresno County whites burned the vacated villages so the Indians would never return. The Humboldt Home Guard, the Hydesville Dragoons, and the Eel River Minutemen roamed northern California seeking to rid the region of "Diggers."

Like the missions, the reservations housed soldiers to keep the Indians in line; each served as a military post for the U.S. Army. Like the missions, the reservations deprived the Indians of their land and forced them to accept another way of life. To discourage Indian traditions, officials prohibited the Miwok from dancing, the Yahi from holding feasts of thanks to the Great Spirit, and the Chumash from wearing long hair and painting their faces. Disobedience meant the withholding of food—a mush of beans and rice—and the consequences were hunger, starvation, disease, and death.

Approximately 10,000 Indians lived on the reservations at various times between 1853 and 1869, but most did not stay long. Hundreds escaped after just a few months' confinement, only to find that their villages were gone and much of their food supply had been destroyed. Of those who stayed on the reservations, 45 percent died of cholera, measles, smallpox, pneumonia, malaria, tuberculosis, or typhoid, many of these diseases brought on or worsened by hunger and malnutrition. Another 15 percent died of syphilis.

Those who survived faced a losing battle with white squatters who moved onto reservation land and were often favored by the "Indian agents" appointed to run the reservations. The squatters diverted water for farming, stole Indian livestock, and built lumber mills that were fed by oak trees whose waste polluted salmon streams. At the Round Valley reservation in 1864 squatters told the Indians to get off the land or be killed. When they refused, forty-five were massacred and the Indian agent in charge allowed the white attackers to remain on the reservation. Eventually, four-fifths of Round Valley was seized by whites, and the white takeover of the other reservations caused them to close by the late 1860s. Anyway, there were hardly any Indians left to confine. In noting the event, Indian commissioner John Ross Browne commented, "So the end of it is here: the reservations are practically abandoned—the remainder of the Indians are being exterminated every day, and the Spanish Mission System has signally failed."

In one last spectacular fight for the right to be a California Indian, the Modoc chose death over civilization. In the early 1860s, they were forced onto a reservation in southern Oregon, which they had to share with Oregon's Klamath Indians. Weary of fighting with the Klamath over reservation lands and food allotments, in 1871 the Modoc left the reservation without permission and returned to their former country along the Lost River in northeastern California. In the winter of 1872–73 a force of a thousand soldiers attacked 150 Modoc and their leader, Kintpuash, whom whites called Captain Jack. He positioned his men in the desolate lava beds of what was by then called Siskiyou County. Whites did not want this land. It was unsuitable for farming or ranching, and further conflict could have been avoided had the Modoc been granted a small portion of the land and left alone. But the local whites refused. The *Yreka Journal* reported that whites were "eager to have the fight go on towards extermination, as there is no safety in trusting such treacherous devils anywhere."

Although heavily outnumbered and fighting with old muzzleloaders and pistols against rifles and artillery, the Modoc put up a heroic fight, killing seventy-five soldiers while suffering few casualties of their own. The army arranged a peace conference, but the Modoc were offered no better terms than a return to the reservation in Oregon. Goaded on by some of his warriors, Chief Kintpuash shot and killed two of the peace negotiators and wounded an Indian agent. The fighting resumed; ultimately the Modoc were defeated, picked off one at a time as they rose from the cover of the lava beds to fire. They were defeated at a cost of half a million dollars. The few survivors were transported to Oklahoma as prisoners of war, and Kintpuash was hanged. Later his grave was robbed and his head was displayed at the Smithsonian Museum in the nation's capital.

In 1864 Jose Chico, a thirty-five-year-old chief of Yokuts in Kern County, wrote a letter to the commander of the federal army in California in which he pleaded for food saying his people were starving to death. As much as any other account, it summarized the experience of California Indians under American rule:

> I am an Indian, and Chief of the Kern River Indians.
> My father was a great chief, and owned all the land on
> the Kern River from the lakes to the tops of the big
> mountains, until the white man came to dig for gold.
> The miners took our women and many of my people
> have died by the whites. . . . The miners laid waste our
> lands and destroyed our means of living. The acorn are
> all gone, and the game is very scarce and hard to get, and
> there is little else to eat than roots and clover. Without
> our land we are starving and are the living dead.

In 1848 there were 125,000 California Indians; in 1860, 35,000; in 1910, 16,000.

Ishi, a Yahi man, believed to be the last
California Indian to live according to the
customs of his people, emerged starving
from the wild in 1911. Given a home by
anthropologists at the University of
California at Berkeley, he revealed a great
deal about the lost culture of the California
Indians. Here, he fires an arrow from a bow
carefully made from a juniper bough.

ISHI 10

HAVING SURVIVED THE GOLD RUSH, the few Chumash still alive during the late nineteenth century lived near white settlements and worked as farm laborers and herdsmen. Having lost their land, the remaining Miwok hired on as fruit pickers and domestic servants. Their work was seasonal and their wages low, but they were still alive and they still thought of themselves as Chumash, Miwok, Yana, and Yahi.

Others didn't. Facing starvation and a bleak future, some Indians moved back to the reservations when they reopened in the early 1870s under the direction of the Methodist Episcopal church. This was part of President Ulysses Grant's new "peace policy," wherein religious leaders were given control over Indians, replacing the corrupt Indian agents. The Methodist ministers in California controlled the supply of food and clothing, and to receive their allotments the reservation Indians had to forsake their culture. Children were forced to attend white-run day schools where they were paddled for speaking Indian languages and practicing Indian customs. When the children were forced to take part in the "outing system," which made them work at low-paying jobs after school, the Indians rebelled by occasionally burning school buildings. It was still wrong to be a California Indian.

Once the luckiest Indians in the world, they had become the most unlucky. Between 1769 and 1910—a span of less than 150 years—12,000 years of life in balance with the land was demolished and the Indians' population had fallen from 400,000 to 16,000. This catastrophe was more than sad. It was monstrous—because it was avoidable. From the moment Father Serra set foot on the beach in San Diego, there was always a choice: to destroy the culture of the California Indians—to kidnap them, enslave them, kill them, and take their land—or just to leave them alone. The California Indians wouldn't have died had calls been heeded to let them be California Indians.

During the period of the missions, Felipe de Neve, the Spanish governor of California from 1775 to 1791, repeatedly criticized the idea that the Indians should be forced to become Spanish. He criticized the missions for exploiting Indian labor and said the Indians should be free to come and go as they pleased. He thought the Indians should become Spanish, but only if they chose to do so, and while governor he tried to stop the building of any new missions, saying the Franciscans treated Indians "worse than slaves."

Neve deplored the deaths of Indians in the missions and eventually refused to send his soldiers after runaways. Any soldier who raped an Indian woman was severely punished, with the offended Indians as witnesses. Neve was usually in conflict with the priests who ran the missions. He believed that civil officials had ultimate authority over the Indians in the missions, and whenever he could he worked to achieve better treatment of the Indians. But as governor he never had authority over them: in 1773 Serra had traveled to Mexico City and persuaded the government to issue a decree stating that "the government, control, and education of the baptized Indians should belong exclusively to the missionaries."

Neve's successor, Governor Diego de Borica, was equally opposed to the missions, remarking that "the treatment given to the Indians in the missions is very harsh and it even reaches the point of cruelty." His successor, Jose Joaquin de Arrillaga, characterized the treatment of Indians as "cruel and tyrannical." And these Spanish governors were not alone in defending the right to be a California Indian.

European philosophers of the Enlightenment—among them Voltaire, Jean-Jacques Rousseau, the Baron de Montesquieu, and Denis Diderot—argued that the Spanish might trade with the Indians but should respect the Indians' way of life, treat them with kindness, and otherwise leave them alone. Voltaire criticized the intolerance of the Catholic church and wrote with contempt about forced conversion to Christianity, saying the church had committed "the monstrous error of persecuting and butchering people in God's name." Rousseau emphasized the natural goodness of men and opposed forced participation in any religion. The Franciscans were well aware of these writers and of the idea that the Indians might be left alone, but they chose to continue the missions. Ultimately, the Enlightenment writers triumphed, as the clamor against the missions finally brought them down in 1834, saving the lives of Indians who had not yet been missionized.

Twenty years later, in a heroic display of courage against a powerful force—the California gold rush—some whites allied themselves with Indians and fought for their rights as human beings. In 1861 George Hanson, the superintendent of Indian affairs in California, called the Indian Indenture Act "a crime against humanity" and expressed outrage at the kidnapping of women and children. As an official of the U.S. government, which was trying to protect peaceful Indians, Hanson fought the slave raiders at every turn, arresting them and freeing their captives.

The *Sacramento Union* denounced the Indenture Act, saying

that Indians were held "as slaves were held in the South; those owning them use them as they please, beat them with clubs and shoot them down like dogs, and no one to say: 'Why do you do so?'" The newspaper said the slave raiders "cut to pieces Indian squaws in their raids for babies." The *Northern Californian* called the Indian Island Massacre of 1860 "a barbaric act of white civilization." The *San Jose News* said Indians were "treated like wolves—robbed, hunted and shot down, without the least provocation—poisoned with the white man's worst diseases."

Although never the majority, these voices spoke loudly and clearly throughout the gold rush to offer an alternative to kidnapping and murder. The most magnificent voice was heard in 1852, when a small group of white lawmakers filed a minority report in the state senate. At the expense of their political careers, they supported the eighteen treaties granting California Indians some land of their own:

> To remove the Indians from this state, we consider impractical. . . . Where else will you locate them? On the desert and sterile regions east of the Sierra Nevada, that they may die of starvation? . . . The policy to us which appears more worthy of a nation whose empire extends from sea to sea, if not one that should seek to raise the character of the Indians, to civilize, refine and enlighten them, should at least be one that could tolerate their existence. . . . Will it be said that the land is not broad enough for them and us? Or that while our doors are open to strangers from all parts of the earth, we have not spare room for the once sole inhabitants of the state? Shall future generations seek in vain for one remaining descendant of the sons of the forest? Has the

love of gold blotted from our minds all feelings of com-
passion and justice?

It can't be said that the forty-niners or the Franciscans didn't
know any better. They decided not to know better although
others told them they should. It can't be said that they were
unaware of the consequences of their actions. They were urged
every day to stop the enslavement and killing. One of their
crimes was to ignore the voices that cried out in behalf of the
California Indians. Another was to believe it was inevitable that
the Indians were all doomed, as Governor Burnett said in 1851,
so the newcomers could be excused for their behavior.

Their greatest crime was to be intolerant of another culture—
to believe that they were civilized and the California Indians
were uncivilized. Under Spanish and American rule, the
California Indians were nearly exterminated because the newcomers believed there was such a thing as "civilization."

Seeing that the Indians wore little clothing and prayed to the
Great Spirit, the Spanish concluded that the natives were uncivilized and had to be changed. Because the Indians gathered their
food and used sticks to dig for vegetables, the forty-niners called
the Indians "Diggers," uncivilized creatures that were to be shot
on sight. Neither group understood that the culture of the
California Indians was just as real to them, and just as meaning-
ful, as the cultures defining the Spanish and the Americans.
Neither group recognized that all people everywhere have a right
to culture and a meaning in life.

As a reminder of what had been lost, history sent a powerful
message to the sons and daughters of the forty-niners, to their
grandchildren, and to generations yet to come. Though few
whites knew it, some California Indians survived into the 1880s,

living in isolated pockets of land beyond the reach of white farmers and ranchers. In the remote area of Mill Creek, east of Red Bluff in northern California, a small band of Yahi struggled against all odds to keep their way of life. By 1911 there was just one of them left—but, remarkably, there *was* one left: a Yahi man, about forty-nine years old, said to be "the last wild Indian" in California. Remarkably, like a postcard from the past, he marched into the twentieth century to provide dramatic proof of what it means to be human and have a culture.

Appropriately, he was crouching in the corral of a slaughterhouse when he was spotted by whites. He expected to be killed, because all his experience told him that contact with whites meant death. Instead, anthropologists took him to the University of California at Berkeley, where he lived for five years until he contracted tuberculosis and died. The anthropologists studied his language, listened to his history, and gave him the name Ishi, which meant "man" in Yahi.

Speaking slowly and sadly, Ishi described the death of his people at the hands of whites. His childhood was a nightmare of bloodshed and death, and his people were always on the move. By 1872, when he was ten, his tribelet had been reduced from 400 people to thirty. Ishi said the thirty entered into what they called "the long concealment," lasting from 1872 to 1884, during which time they had no contact with whites and covered up all traces of their existence. They walked on rocks and waded down rivers for miles so they wouldn't leave any footprints. They crawled through rabbit trails cut into thick brush and traveled under cover of darkness whenever whites got too close to their campsite. Forced out of the long concealment by starvation, they often raided farms and ranches, but by 1894 the band was down to five: Ishi, his mother and sister, and two other men. They retreated from Mill Creek to Deer Creek, the only place left to hide, and when Ishi's mother died in 1908 he was the last of his people left. He lived alone in the wilderness for three years, until his loneliness became unbearable. The saddest moment of his life in the white world came when the anthropologists asked him if he would go back to Mill Creek and show them how the Yahi lived. He did not want to go. The thought of home made him cry.

The last five years of his life were happy because he was allowed to be a Yahi, and the people who met him and knew him came to understand how precious that was to him. They marveled at his patience in making the tools he lived by; they watched him spend nearly two weeks making a bow from juniper, cutting it, shaving it, soaking it, and bending it to just the right angle for a perfect balance. They came to see that the arrows and salmon spears he made were not just things he possessed but were a part of him, what he was. He was kind, courteous, and generous, and nothing made him happier than to be able to give something away—his arrowheads and spear points and even bows. His good manners and respect were especially evident in the company of women. He never initiated a conversation with a woman, and whenever a woman spoke to him he answered politely but without looking directly at her, in the Yahi way.

Ishi was neat and orderly, and his clothes, toilet articles, and other possessions were carefully spaced on the shelves in his small room. In his clothes box he kept a bar of scented soap and a can of talcum powder, which he called lady powder. These were among his greatest treasures and he never used them. He learned to write his name but wouldn't speak it. He bathed every day, plucked out his facial hair, and was careful to sleep so the moon couldn't shine on his face. He continued to make soup in the Yahi way and conserved every scrap of food, even eating the

salmon bones to please the Great Spirit. He never touched anything that was not his; whenever a stranger touched or misplaced
his belongings, he showed his displeasure by becoming anxious
and fidgety but never voiced disapproval and never spoke the
stranger's name.

The people who knew him said he was cheerful, patient, con-
tented, and balanced, and never given to anger. He never volun-
teered criticism of the white man's ways, but when pressed he
offered his opinion. He considered the white man to be inventive
and very clever but lacking in proper reserve and in an under-
standing of nature and life. Ishi never seemed confused, never
seemed in search of anything, never seemed lost, and never seemed
in a hurry. That was because he knew who he was—Yahi—and it
brought meaning to his life.

EPILOGUE

URING THE LATE NINETEENTH CENTURY, with the aid of sympathetic whites, California Indians fought to get their land back and to retain their culture. The national Indian Rights Association was formed in 1882. The Sequoya League was created in 1901, and it succeeded in getting land for Indians in the San Diego area. After nearly twenty-five years of lobbying, in 1924 Indians were made citizens of the United States, partly because of their heroic service in World War I.

During the 1920s a dozen Indian organizations, from the Mission Indian Federation to the Indian Brotherhood, campaigned for legislation to compensate California Indians for the 1851–52 treaty lands. The California legislature authorized the attorney general to act on behalf of the California Indians and sue the federal government for compensation. The complex law suit that followed lasted sixteen years; finally, in 1944, the U.S. Court of Claims awarded California Indians $5 million for the land promised in the earlier treaties. This amounted to less than a dollar an acre for the land lost under the eighteen treaties.

This modest sum satisfied neither the Indians nor their white allies. During the 1940s and 1950s more than twenty separate lawsuits were filed to gain compensation for the loss of the California lands not included in the eighteen treaties of 1851–52. A settlement was reached in 1963: the California Indians were awarded $29 million for their aboriginal claim to the state. By 1972 the U.S. secretary of the interior had approved a list of more than 69,000 California Indians, each of whom received a payment of approximately $700.

In addition to money, the California Indians gradually got some of their land back. Beginning in 1906, Congress passed a series of acts granting reserves of land to tribes; by 1950 a total of 117 Indian communities had been established on lands owned by the federal government or purchased by the government for Indians. They varied in size from a one-acre plot in Yuba County to the Hoopa reservation in Humboldt County, with over 116,000 acres. The Indian Reorganization Act of 1934 gave California Indians more control over reservation businesses, provided loans to stimulate their economies, and improved health and education services.

Since the 1920s the population of the California Indians, like that of other Native American groups, has continued to rise. In 1990 there were approximately 80,000 Californians descended from the Indians who had been living in the state in 1848. Many California Indians now live in urban areas and have become integrated into white society. Others continue to live on tribal lands and take care to preserve their culture. The Atsugewi still use their knowledge of native medicines and foods in their daily lives. The Yurok still fish for salmon in the Klamath River. The Pomo still follow their traditional religion and rely on shamans for ancient curing practices. The Pomo also host an annual spring festival featuring traditional dances, games, costumes, and food. In 1987 the Pomo and representatives from other California tribes protested a campaign in the Roman Catholic church to make Father Serra a saint.

CHRONOLOGY

10,000 B.C. Native Americans enter California.

1542 Juan Rodriguez Cabrillo (Spain) explores the California coast.

1579 Sir Francis Drake (England) explores Bodega Bay.

1595 Sebastian Rodriguez Cermeno (Spain) anchors in San Francisco Bay.

1602 Sebastian Vizcaino (Spain) visits Monterey Bay.

1769 Sacred expedition. Junipero Serra (Spain) founds Mission San Diego.

1770 San Carlos Borromeo de Carmelo established.

1771 San Gabriel and San Antonio de Padua established.

1772 San Luis Obispo established.

1773 California Indians placed under the control of Franciscans.

1775 San Diego burned; Father Luis Jayme killed.

1776 San Juan Capistrano and San Francisco established.

1777 Santa Clara established.

1782 San Buenaventura established.

1784 Death of Serra. Fermin Lasuen succeeds Serra.

1786 Santa Barbara established.

1787 La Purisima Concepcion established.

1791 Santa Cruz and Soledad established.

1797 San Jose, San Juan Bautista, San Miguel Arcángel, and San Fernando Rey established.

1798 San Luis Rey established.

1804–06 Meriwether Lewis and William Clark (U.S.) explore the American West, reaching the Pacific Ocean.

1804 Santa Inés established.

1806 Measles epidemic in the missions.

1812 Russians establish Fort Ross in northern California.

1817 San Rafael established. Syphilis epidemic in San Francisco.

1821 Mexico wins independence from Spain; assumes control of California.

1823 Solano established.

1827 Measles epidemic in the missions.

1834 Secularization of the missions begins.

1841–42 John Charles Fremont (U.S.) explores California.

1842 Russians abandon Fort Ross.

1846–48 Mexican-American War.

1848 Treaty of Guadalupe Hidalgo signed, ending Mexican-American War; United States assumes control of California. Discovery of gold begins California gold rush.

1850 California becomes 31st state. Indian Indenture Act becomes law. Clear Lake Massacre.

1850–51 Mariposa War between miners and Miwok and Yokuts.

1851–52 Eighteen California Indian treaties signed.

1852 U.S. Senate rejects the eighteen treaties. Trinity River Massacre.

1853 Smith River Massacre. Congress establishes five reservations for California Indians. Forced removal of Indians by white militias begins.

1860 Indian Island Massacre.

1869 Transcontinental railroad completed.

1872–73 Modoc War.

1882 Indian Rights Association formed.

1906–50 Congress passes series of acts granting reserves of land to California Indian tribes.

1911 Ishi joins the white world.

1916 Death of Ishi.

1924 Indians made citizens of the United States.

1944 California Indians awarded $5 million for land promised under the eighteen treaties of 1852.

1963 California Indians awarded $29 million for aboriginal claims.

GLOSSARY OF SELECTED CALIFORNIA INDIAN TRIBAL NAMES

Achomawi	Ah-cho-mah´-wee	Modoc	Mo´-dock
Alliklik	Al-lik´-lik	Mojave	Mo-hav´-vee
Atsugewi	At-su-gay´-wee	Monache	Mo-nah´ chee
Cahto	Kah´-to	Nongatl	Non´-gatl
Cahuilla	Kah-wee´-yah	Paiute	Pie-yoot´
Chemehuevi	Chem-eh-way´-vee	Pomo	Po´-mo
Chilula	Chil-lu´-lah	Salinan	Sal-leen´-nan
Chimariko	Chih-mair´-ih-ko	Serrano	Ser-rah´-no
Chumash	Choo´-mash	Shasta	Shas´-ta
Costanoan	Cost-ah-no´-an	Shoshone	Sho-sho´-nee
Cupeño	Coo-pay´-nyo	Sinkyone	Sink´-yoan
Diegueño	Dee-eh-gay´-nyo	Tolowa	Toe´-lo-wah
Esselen	Ess´-sel-len	Tübatulabal	Too-bah´-too-lah-bal
Fernandeño	Fer-nan-day´-nyo	Vanyume	Van-yoo´-mee
Gabrieleno	Gab-ree-al-ay´-nyo	Wailaki	Wy´-lak-kee
Halchidhoma	Hal-chid´-do-mah	Wappo	Wahp´-po
Hupa	Hoo´-pah	Washo	Wah´-sho
Juaneño	Wahn-ayn´-nyo	Whilkut	Whil´-koot
Kamia	Kah´-mee-ya	Wintun	Win-toon´
Karok	Kah´-rock	Wiyot	Wee´-yot
Kawaiisu	Kah-wy´-ih-soo	Yahi	Yah´-hee
Kitanemuk	Kih-tan´-nee-muk	Yana	Yah´-nah
Lassik	Las´-sik	Yokuts	Yo´-koots
Luiseño	Loo-is-ay´-nyo	Yuki	Yoo´-kee
Maidu	My´-doo	Yuma	Yoo´-mah
Mattole	Mat-toal´	Yurok	Yur´-ock
Miwok	Mee´-wock		

Source: Heizer & Elsasser, *The Natural World of the California Indian*, 1980.

BIBLIOGRAPHIC NOTE

INFORMATION RELATING TO THE CULTURE of California Indians before 1769 was drawn from the following sources: Bruce W. Barton, *The Tree at the Center of the World: A Story of the California Missions* (Santa Barbara, Calif.: Ross Erikson Publishers, 1980); Robert F. Heizer and Albert B. Elsasser, *The Natural World of the California Indian* (Berkeley, Calif.: University of California Press, 1980); Robert F. Heizer and M. A. Whipple (eds.), *The California Indians: A Source Book* (Berkeley, Calif.: University of California Press, 1971); C. L. Keyworth, *California Indians* (New York: Facts on File, 1991); George Harwood Phillips, *The Enduring Struggle: Indians in California History* (San Francisco: Boyd and Fraser, 1981); and James J. Rawls, *Indians of California: The Changing Image* (Norman, Okla.: University of Oklahoma Press, 1984).

Population estimates for the New World are derived from Henry F. Dobyns, "Estimating Aboriginal American Population: An appraisal of Techniques with a Hemispheric Estimate," *Current Anthropology*, VII (1966), pp. 395-416; Wilber Jacobs, "The Tip of an Iceberg: PreColumbian Indian Demography and Some Implications for Revisionism," *William and Mary Quarterly* (1974) pp. 123-32; David E. Stannard, *American Holocaust: The Conquest of the New World* (New York: Oxford University Press, 1992); and Russell Thornton, *American Indian Holocaust and Survival: A Population History Since 1492* (Norman, Oklahoma: University of Oklahoma Press, 1987).

Information concerning the Indians under Spanish and Mexican rule came from Edward D. Castillo, "The Impact of Euro-American Exploration and Settlement," pp. 99–126 of Robert F. Heizer (ed.), *Handbook of North American Indians,* Volume 8 (Washington, D.C.: Smithsonian Institution, 1978); Charles C. Colley, "The Missionization of the Coast Miwok Indians of California," *California*

Historical Society Quarterly, June 1970, pp. 143–61; Sherburne F. Cook, *The Conflict Between the California Indian and White Civilization* (Berkeley, Calif.: University of California Press, 1943); Rupert Costo and Jeannette Henry (eds.), *The Missions of California: A Legacy of Genocide* (San Francisco: Indian Historian Press, 1987); Daniel Fogel, *Junipero Serra, the Vatican and Enslavement Theology* (San Francisco: ISM Press, 1988); Maynard Geiger, O.F.M. (ed.), *Franciscan Missionaries in Hispanic California, 1769–1848: A Biographical Dictionary* (San Marino, Calif.: Huntington Library, 1969); Maynard Geiger, O.F.M., *The Indians of Mission Santa Barbara in Paganism and Christianity* (Santa Barbara, Calif.: Mission Santa Barbara, 1960); Maynard Geiger, O.F.M., *Mission Santa Barbara, 1782–1965* (Santa Barbara, Calif.: Franciscan Fathers of California, 1965); Francis F. Guest, O.F.M., "Junipero Serra and His Approach to the Indians," *Southern California Quarterly,* Fall 1985, pp. 223–61; Robert F. Heizer and Alan J. Almquist, *The Other Californians: Prejudice and Discrimination Under Spain, Mexico and the United States to 1920* (Berkeley, Calif.: University of California Press, 1971); George Harwood Phillips, *Indians and Intruders in Central California, 1769–1849* (Norman, Okla.: University of Oklahoma Press, 1993); and Florence C. Shipek, "California Indian Reactions to the Franciscans," *The Americas,* April 1985, pp. 480–91.

Information concerning the gold rush, the reservations, and the struggle for compensation came from Todd Benson, "The Consequences of Reservation Life: Native Californians on the Round Valley Reservation, 1871–1884," *Pacific Historical Review,* May 1991, pp. 221–44; Lynwood Carranco and Estle Beard, *Genocide and Vendetta: The Round Valley Wars of Northern California* (Norman, Okla.: University of Oklahoma Press, 1981); Robert Chandler, "The Failure of Reform: White Attitudes and Indian Responses in California During the Civil War Era," *Pacific Historian,* Fall 1980, pp. 284–94; Robert F. Heizer and Alan J. Almquist, *The Other Californians: Prejudice and Discrimination Under Spain, Mexico and the United States to 1920* (Berkeley, Calif.: University of California Press, 1971); Albert L. Hurtado, *Indian Survival on the California Frontier* (New

Haven, Ct.: Yale University Press, 1988); Jack Norton, *Genocide in Northwestern California* (San Francisco: Indian Historian Press, 1979); and George Harwood Phillips, *Chiefs and Challengers: Indian Resistance and Cooperation in Southern California* (Berkeley, Calif.: University of California Press, 1975).

Ishi's life is recounted in Theodora Kroeber, *Ishi in Two Worlds: A Biography of the Last Wild Indian in North America* (Berkeley, Calif.: University of California Press, 1961), and Robert F. Heizer and Theodora Kroeber (eds.), *Ishi the Last Yahi: A Documentary History* (Berkeley, Calif.: University of California Press, 1979).

Teachers Katherine Freeburg and Kay Lunine, and librarians Elizabeth Overmyer and Judy Turner, provided valuable criticisms of the manuscript. Some quotations were edited for clarity.

INDEX

Page numbers in **boldface** refer
to illustrations.

PICTURE CREDITS